D0720531

DRAGON CONVERSATION

DRAGON CONVERSATION

(TALKS WITH A QUARTER SENTINEL)

by

JOE DUVERNAY

poetic fiction

Copyright ©2000 by Joe Duvernay
All rights reserved.
No part of this book may be reproduced, stored in a retrieval
system, or transmitted by any means, electronic mechanical,
photocopying, recording, or otherwise, without written
permission from the author.

ISBN: 1-58721-562-4

1stBook – rev. 9/15/00

ABOUT THE BOOK

The book is a work of poetry. I have allowed two fictional characters to open and close the work. The one is the 'bringer' of poems "The Fifth Quarter Sentinel" described herein, the other is the interviewer. The poems are what one poet thinks and feels about our time.

I hope that this work offends none and that something read in the work affects the reader positively.

CONTENTS

DRAGON DIALOGUE I

FACES AT REST II

AUTHORS NOTE

Refer to, 'Who am I' as explanation!

Readers Being Choregus

stared at that scene more than can say.
Day upon day, when there.
Tympanum told,
sentially without end
down twice narrow path strode they,
sometimes diagonally of what knew,
often straight,
which was challenge plenty.
Torii of the oldest pine,
gateway conceived,
head or two cleaved,
trachyte garden wall built with.

Land ho!
There! Off starboard
see advance trailings,
notice leavings targeted by
they who little have.
One man's this, another's that, et al.

PRELUDE

Follows...description of a character in first book "I Begin".
Where, in poem 'Bell Subject' we first met...
A Quarter sentinel allows no quarter be given at one far end of undertakings.
Guards gate to quarter given. More possibly tiring invention, Poetic Fiction.

The Quarter sentinel? Explained thus to they that know not of the post.

       Quarter Sentinel uses time differently.
       Decades often are commandeered, shoved in with,
       up against a future or previous one.
The Mix-up, the mix-in and thankfully.
       Higher-archy
       Hydrogen
       Noble numbered
       Hydrogen
       Dot matrix
       Higher Archy
       Hydrogen
       Noble now and again.
       First-mixer
       Hydrogen
Dot Matrix
       Wave Fulfillment
       Dot matrix
       Universal Variant
       Galaxy Intonement
       Quadrant Exercise

Quarter Sentinel -
       Gate Keeper
       Threat Leaver
       Text Reader
       Head Cleaver

Neat! Either or!
Comments on same…"in the second Dot Matrix lies the jewels".
Self.
Redundant!
Born of these!
The accommodation of individuals collapses.
The argument adds and negates all
at level of the individual
everything is due,
hence only random may decide.

LOG READ! …Signal-in.:

……………………………

Sig-in.: …Interview with the Fifth Quarter Sentinel
Sig-in.: …A.D. 3000
Sig-in.: …S.P.O.T.S. Base NINE (Spontaneous Positioning
          Of/In Time Sequencing)
Sig-in.: …Minor Moon FOUR
Sig-in.: …Saturn Proper
Sig-in.: …Interviewer, Seti Prime, t.t.p. (Topic topper
          professional)

……………………………
……………………………

INTERVIEW READ!…

………………………

Rd-t.t.p-in.: …"Why have you come
                and with what stories?"
Rd-QS-in.: … "Born in a year of the Dragon!
                So, you are brought Dragon Tales.
                Dragon talks…'Figure cut by these noble
                beasts, in minds eye, is passing well lit.
                Mammoth Expenditures of Invention!
                …I remember Saint George the slayer.
                The dragon of putting down the sword.
                Dragon of a saving grace, that graces all.
                …same desires as before!
                And because, liking the dragons many
                symbolism's
                long before hearing of some supposed
                connection
                to God averse, last days phenomena…leaves
                me
                cold-forged to my way…Level poetry
                follows!"
Rd-t.t.p-in.: …"Why the Fifth?"

Rd-QS-in.: ... "Because though you started your latest count
from the time of His death and are now at 3000,
the First Quarter Sentinel was positioned nearly
2,000,000 years ago, when all here was baboon or
Australopithecine.
The First of my kind being fully realized and
assigned the Special Chore - To watch over actions
produced by Earth's inhabitants with an eye to what
via your much valued Free Will, is encompassed in
your yes and no. To guard the door to Quarter given.
Obviously, if left entirely to man's devices, Earth
that jewel of a planet would now be non-existent.
The job is getting harder, but *my* yes and no
counterbalance some of your bad decisions."
Rd-t.t.p-in.: ... "Not all?"
And what is the average life-span of a Sentinel?
Rd-QS-in.: ... "You'll mark I mentioned your Free Will.
This one
of Random's set-pieces cannot be pre-determined
or easily interfered with, though there have been
instances.... ----. Sorry! Almost left my post!
Leave it! Perhaps we'll breach this subject
another time."
Rd-t.t.p-in.: ... "the life-span?"
Rd-QS-in.: ... "That is left to His whim. But I can tell you
it is long,
it varies and I am the Fifth.
Shall we trace on?"
Rd-t.t.p-in.: ... "Please!"

DRAGON

DIALOGUE

I

STILL SELFISH

In this world…
Because you know your ancestry
You have no searchers here!

You may be hamstrung in this race,
Because you don't know your ancestry
or are discovering it!

Of course, all had, at some point to discover it
…so reluctantly, all are included!

Most of our names go back many tractable centuries.
First names and last.

Now! If your namesakes were all murderers or doctors
or priests or writers or slaves ..do that which beckons,
that which calls from what depths.
In the swim or 'against the grain'.
        Again, make it your choice.

This one, does cringe when we say 'mine' or 'I' a lot!
I do it too…
Stay innocent enough to, never care much
if you win over me, because you may need it more than myself
And I may be on the watch for same,
having found a new way to gather strength!

OF CRYING

Hoist the flag of what makes me cry!

I'll tell you!
Obviously strong men, committed men, who when
retiring from a long and storied career, as coach for
instance,
he breaks into tears and the respect and tears given him by
his men,
and all of it makes us better!
Or when after long abuse and torment or recognition neither
sought-out
nor found, one is recognized as hero and, at base, good man
only now,
when in silence, he always was.
Only when men of such strength who never are seen with
tear in eye
nor cry in heart, are reduced to such basic human emotion
as tears allow,
am I brought to tears. Or when the honest, ethical thing is
done, consequences
be damned.

Witness tears of joy or sorrow that would not be held back by
idea of self,
of how to be a man and you become, in a moment, more than or
as much as a man.

And all the rallying and cheering captured by the disquiet
in someone's
helping hand, is tossed in the toilet, along with all the
detritus of the day,
that must be,
if survival is eminent, thrown away.
These opposites too make up a day!

KU

Are they wrong?
They treat themselves like kings and queens, in their own homes,
in their minds, their hearts.
In those bodies of theirs…the play of sunlight on the brow,
is direct
cause of the 14 hour a day squint they make.
Is world still so undiscovered by them, that they should
squint so?
>   Well of course the answer is yes and will always be
>   yes,
>   For the world calls it's own plays…
>   Over the tops of those made by our will.
And any simile that appears is made by all…it appears!

FUSS

Talking about clear road ahead!
Intuit crossing event horizon in two directions.
No bleeding diary.
Some cleaverence aeh!
      By categorizing, we know what to call a thing!
By categorizing, we take the future from all of us!
We take Our planet, our stars, et al.
we few, we white men.
      It is good to prob.
It is in interest to know.
But doing such things as going beneath the Ice
and seeking to know in an instant, what should seek
to be known only after much time is spent is another - our technology,
we can do it, rush right in mistake…and if not this, the drilling almost certainly is.
      Simply must lock hands, minds and hearts with earth
      simple peoples!
They must be in boardroom too!
Because in them reside all the brushed aside as unneeded, primitive
Feel and knowing, the standing still and sensing with given instruments of
how to treat Ma Earth.
      This Universal heritage belongs to all Earth's inhabitants,
      not just some.
We have no permission to place satellites in orbit,
nuclear weapons in ground, nor trees in box cars!
We do not agree with the dividing up of peoples and places,
with the taking that has been done.
      Now! To know how to follow, to let go, is quality
      needed so badly,
that it would never cross mind, because it smacks of lost control.
Imagine breathing easy for a year or two!
Our developed infrastructure you think will fall

if not given constant attention.
"Those non-builders, those users will destroy everything!"
Well I think not!   Builders there too!   And lo!   Perhaps some things need destroying,
need bringing down,
need restructuring!
I'll not call their names to you here,
their balance will be found in times dutiful hand.
But please note…
life is once removed from the most miracle of all events,
the life of God within and without this escaped chance.
Where slope is equal to drop
And ninth life is under-pinned with opting out.
Where time is long and moment sharp
in milestone building, in time-line art.

SOME HISTORY

What up in nat! Yeah Boyee!
I Know you no.
I sow, I sow!
I salsa!
"A Cavaeyo!"
Besa segurdo!
Besa maguiro!
es loco!
A travieyo!

Sow seed sown by men of such rank and rancor and respect and tanker like
resolve to preserve and protect this my Mother, my Father thing this WWII
fought for and again yet placed in the middle with my 'cross and twice
  baroque', American generation speak and trawllian be-
  mooring.
Grandfather horseshoeing and fighting for the WWI effort,
a fair ferrier he.
While during the fortunate for some "War' in Vietnam, my younger brother served.
And again during the fortunate for some, unfortunate for all Gulf War
  crises my Son est Served.

Love the idea of crossing boundaries erected by our un-sure,
rightness of the thing. As for me,
Was told more than once, trying, with a family in tow to
Join the Vietnam Affair, quilt mounting, that I should continue doing the
work I was doing for and with Western Electric.
Recall my Draft Lottery number was something like 365.
It was a stunning discovery then as now and an occurrence
crafted obliquely yet, by my frightened will.

We football players, we high-school stars were all scared
back then,
because letters were in the mail and some were going to jail,
while others were accounting their special daddy privileges and
still others
skipped to another country to wait out their forgetting.
While others still, with little means and no one to stand for them
and say no
Were on their way to and in war.
Find myself saying these things here as hopeful purging from
being
of this locked-in failure feel.
Simply was not called!
But I spy that I'am called now.
Called to write down our misshapen misgivings about our
numbered views
of this reality this.

Subdued by self to create paper words and flying meanings.
These walking metaphors and trying seasons of a soul.
What is asked of multiple universes and people of short sight is
that we use
all of our resources, even seemingly quiet ones to equip our total
           winning.   Wherein all the answers are on the table,
           because all of the
           questions are taken-up, branded with our humane
           mark
and discussed by all.
Where no fray is left un-entered.
Where no task is found de-natured.

THE PEOPLE

Every unknown source is confounded with irony as the wealth
grows long.
Over bare and darkly night, monuments force and fade and
follow broken slants of
straw men and women, and no manner of special privilege will
convey the wanted
winnings that lie dormant there.

Cater to the best that lives with the worst and know that this is
so!
Follow, don't follow!
All quiet the same.
                    Even a trued-up game.
And broken windows are all fixed.
And no more, as cry in the land, is heard…soft moan of our fear.
His fear Her fear.
And no less… There ---> fear.
Don't wish to be too hard on you!
AH! The fool enters hearty.
Philosopher is caught with 1984 personal computer, with e-prom
escarpments
where fishes moan too.
And he dies many times. As each tree falls he knows and feels it
and pieces of him fly away!
The salvation sought… The crown in the jewel… For chief
certain!
This I know…
I fear not knowing you and first principles abandoned!
                    But too let it be said…
This fear, this ---> Not fear.
Don't let that scare you!
Don't let that let you think that my stake in the game is
                    devalued defaced strengthened cross wired and found
                    with likely
torrent of admiration and admonishment, between sheets of

spilled coins and
announced curfews for returning them.

Ever a-pace races run ad-continuum.
Astride faces welcoming changes.
Traces of your scent.
> Foundlings ranked up there with the most.
> Non-confused.
> Training privileges.
> Able to read book, enjoy concert,
> And exact all the misuse applicable.
> Able to hear of your plight elsewhere in the world,
> but improperly embarked to guarantee you food and
> water… must fix this!

KATANA

By way of anticipation…your left there as it was.
Thy fine edge seen in the light of any light.
Not noticed in the dark and bright.
Arms, legs, torso, neck and head hardly visible.
Wagnerian day long lament.
Takaeda, Ueshiba Sensei
before this and Shioda Sensei
and Obata Sensei - est D.

Foolish remembering that has one separated
from the overweaning method of display
attracted to and still from,
Way of that thing had.
With voice of song, touch of lightening,
splitting asunder, ahead does make way.
All does make way. In thought through.
In sought, few.

And the using, cleaning and stroking.
Intimacy had now and then,
Both of field and without.
Short cuts made with Short Sword.
Shorter still with near over-large blade…Tanto!
And tsuba and hilt may take a life without doubt.
Cut through, as an excellent stance and 'cut come from' is
achieved.
Over head, under head, all are best,
but a few here too, will decide the day as always,
as bent, we are acquired, achieved of our goal.

And always fight with battodo, Musashi's mistakes and choices.
Conan's repetitious expenditures.
Tarl Cabot's relieved re-tellings.
And the Executioners immediacy.
A Through cut, a severed parts several.

A half man found. More half men.
This Blade has a taste for Rightness.
As set aside after long days battle,
As come astride, the arm-chair near
then far back from the fire.
As handed over at silk-worms pace,
As attracted backward, as separate space.

VAGUELY EXPERIENCED OPPOSITE?
THE PEOPLE II, A TRIBUTE

Not specifically, but generally,
dutch were ruthless
english regal
french caring.
As on wings of colonies drawn and quartered,
they created their new worlds…
spanish, portuguese were heretical with what they
and Catholicism hammered into people.

Now, there is enough for all.
Their were African tribes that speakable
and unspeakable things 'do' to one another.
Asians that cannot hide from excess
And people of the Americas that were quite a lot
of conquerors.
And we have c-span, de tocqueville
un beaumont.
And 'early America and breaking for dinner to hear speeches by many
politicians of this or that assembly.'
Names of appointance come up
names like Robespierre, exactimon!
…and Hugo let me in.!.
drawing the blind-lion part, by a string,
a rope burned into scull's memory.
When one feels older than you know you are,
much older, have lived in-numerable times.
Have seen your black and white coming and going.
Your building toward and out of race-war skeptics.
An un-certified course of study and action.
Something it were best our young knew not!

Their truth is sifted, dispatched,
watched under strobe-light microscopes,

that show angles thought to be extinct,
that in turn deliver un-seen sights,
that might...carry their own scenes quite well!
Except that tell and craft convinced economy that
Enough was not quite enough after all.
Exactimon!

INTERVIEW READ!...
....
Rd-t.t.p.-in: ..."Forgive me! But how does this figure in?"
Rd-QS-in.: ... "It doesn't!"

WEEKENDS

Not too much,
On Sundays.
Even less on Saturdays.
My thought...to rest.
To do what I will...
No tooth brush to scrape,
No razor to shave,
No comb near this head.
Soap? Hands only.
None of this business week norm!
More industrial martial arts practice and exercise.
Only reading what pulls at this T-shirt's collarless.
No driving in vehicle.
No morning donut, sometimes no coffee.
No hasty, unremarkable lunch.
Cooking for self and occasionally a friend.

Only what I desire...
a Saturday that lays there,
a Sunday that walks slow,
my laundry day.
And in-between...salsa radio Saturday night,
Meet The Press, CBS Sunday Morning, Booknotes
and what written, from what has attenuated.

You'd better rest at a hurried pace!
You know too much to go all weekend long too.
Fall back, drop out of line, give up!
The world can spare you for a time!

Your choice.
Your singular voice.
Un-song when sung.
Un-gone when done.

INTERVIEW READ!...
....
Rd-QS-in.: ..."I only relay the words!"
         "Patience!"

POOR PROTEST

Feel so raped at thought of mother earth exposed,
drilled, siphoned and put in air.
I buy!
I drive to work and back and hither and yon!
I fly unannounced into sly moon!
I sigh and shake head as pounced by our ego-away!
I'am guilty!

Holes we have dug alone,
are enough to pass sentence disastrous!
That hollow sound of 'what will the earth do now?
She, poor dear has many entry points of foreign matter.
Un-wanted sums.
Dead things sprung.
A stirring of what should not be stirred.
         An opening of what should have stayed
         locked.
Rock poured where it is not wanted.
Cache of obsessions fashioned after completely blind
desires.

But still a chance, while sky is some blue.
         Victory dance, for you saving few.
Gratifying announcement of less toxins in the air.
         Near-lost approach of real caring dare.

WHAT TO CALL IT

Dragon dialogue is tenderly conspicuous today.
Oh yeah! Episodes with 'conscripted air' are softly spoken,
as if they were not there!
Un the monster comes through the walls again!
'That while there are alternatives,
it can surely be said, there are none.'

And there you reside and slide up down in and out all
noises there!
Safely having slide into second,
third a bust-loose away.
Home plate? You would know of home plate?
Home plate is such that it can be repeated three times close
and wanted even more.

TO THE FLEETING AND THE CAUGHT

Thoughts lost in tense-smoke air
A jewelry fantasticated day-by dare.
There is too much time…
shoved under book-piles, under tables
over me, over youe.
This explains the I that speaks is man!

I listen close, deep in the silence
of each vehicles passing, on road below.
Sound is not un-like waves crashing on a shore.
Oh! The too few words trick.
Which is not a trick at all.
Instead a coming forward
a standing to - po

Thoughts rammed in from some outside force
from one ampled source and many and
Sure I didn't want you around…
for your good, rarely for mine.

See while I admit to
and shy from what thought all along.
That a woman is best off away from this one.
This one is strong - so plying.
Believes with some countenance
in What John Norman could teach,
of beauty, respect and only you do to you,
most contumely too is self inflicted.
Chanced bying!

WARNING!…
……..Channel Attenuation!…
……Shift!… …………

FREE GIFTS

The long view through the clouds.
Not noticed by kids playing games below.
Or by cat scampering across lawn.
Nor by you in your in-doors escape
or too early, mid-day yawn.

But, there it is…
way through that patch to the one beyond.
A variety not captured by any another day
at any other hour.
Yours aplenty.
On the run.

PROFFERED AMBIGUITY

Said he had a lock on life.
Knew all the answers.
Questions not asked were unimportant.
Soil and rock not pressed by his feet,
wondered why they were left out.
Where his eyes did not fall, empty darkness ensued.
Women once cared for, said goodby to.
Family that has given and taken so much,
were shelved as he escaped what he thought passed as mire.
Books left for a more opportune time were read.
Songs sung with gusto and joy,

were closed off in unlighted, dank basements,
left on some shore.
Winds sway of branches,
brought no pleasure.
Emptiness made full.
Charge, to sit quiet, rescinded.

And so,
Give-up realizations so long guarded
by select inputs.
No more sitting alone wasting a life lived.
Still not interested in most company kept.
Will he cease cutting his hair?
Will it grow into a 'future-in-poetry' bought.
Bought while the store was open
bought when all the lights were out.
Purchased with empty hole as spout.
Or given, as payment is extracted by the blessing
as its due.
The project is 'to write what can't be articulated'.
Said a Tennyson in a similar way.
Try despite obstacles hard by...
Grow up a bad good man as love screams for more and sighs.

Whispers not heard, while listening closely.
Intentions disturbed with the brewing by witches.
Which church is ours? Which shirt towers?
Make your choice the piercing reflection of how short it is
and how little time is left. How ridiculous is
                    crying, holding and hiding and sighing.
          Is there intent to help, or is it simply waiting out it's
time?

WISHES NOT WASTED

Can see the pass from here,
though it is but a slight trace
in its ten miles away!
Wishing on a star place, sacred to life of Earth.
The trees lend themselves to our passing.
To our standing near them.
Grass loves a hoof as much as the foot.
Not every yesterday is forgotten.
Nor are all sorrows knocking.
Many have abandoned task,
under our long ago not letting in.

A firm stance…
in the light of these palm-tree like musings.
Lost worker,
inside this appointed slavery.
A hero petrified,
not by what is there upon looking,
but by what will come if I do not.
A two tomorrow's choicest leavings
taken as manna…to last forever,
as I pray, high and wide…

With a hubris that contains all fears.
With a melancholy that's lasted the years.
With a strange thought given straight out.
For modern mind, on wishing route.

WHO AM I

Being both, could never, except very early on,
recognize what side I belonged on, because it was always both.
         Black and White... Brown Green Yellow and Red

It is a matter of ancestry, not forgotten or hidden
or thrown away. Achieved!
So as I operate on self,
in the mystical mistaken idea that I can affect positively,
It is remembered that only two hands have I,
And to operate on self, takes more than that.
It takes all the towns and villages.
Every hut and shanty.
All your rich mans' joys and treasures.
all the butts and panties.
Every unexpected sip it measures.

Each way of seeing things.
All the days asking praise.

About to enter lost city...
bankrupt attitude un-sconced...
assured!
As opposite welcomed aboard.

A NEW WORD

Is all artistry some kind of pain revealed?
Of loss
of near
of unwakened wanting ear,
here near, where we sear steaks cut
just now?

All the entry had on both sides of our equation.

Elsewhere! Believers arrive at back of building,
as waved off they skip over starboard deck,
Plain out of sight and splash their souls as they
slip below the surface. For all to see no less!

There are days when you can't find me,
No matter how hard you try.
There are ways to be invisible,
If only you'd buy…the scheme that leaves our surrival.

NO UNSEEN WEDDING YET

Today, it won't let me leave!
Am strapped to writing chair.
Held down about shoulders
by unseen welcomed quests,
clammering about for a word in edge-wise.
That would have their tears fall,
hear their tongues spoken.
…Escape back from it all.

Out comes, 'Welcomed quests, please note.
That today on the occasion so blessed,
of my daughters wedding in-tacit
approval of forms and customs acquired and relieved,
I do herewith invite and ignite you to your best behaviors
and gentlemanly and lady-like endeavors to watch and weigh clear,
the sharpened moments that follow…
A father is pleased'.

IF ONLY TO SEE

Where I sit here in my garret
it's so beautiful, the sky, the mountain, the forest,
that I must work at some wondrous expectant
work.
Something that too gains.
No emptiness, anywhere to be found.
All full.

NO RESCUE

A ladder climbing to the stars
Soft landing on many Mars.
Taken measure, likeness drawn close,
escape from attention,
another lost art rescued.
A toast!

A drive down the boulevard Van Nuys,
Try Ventura as sight for sore eyes.
Manic depression let in,
Then chewed by a desire to conquer all sin.

Some moments contuse,
act right in your shoes and say that
right is right and good, good,
when you find it so.
And only the 'not awake today' will not listen,
as their plight is revealed to them.
That they will not win.
That there is little to no hope,
that their floundering and making some spectacle,
will be allowed return…
they are lost and gladly wasted
Upon the heap that scraps.
Detritus. Ignite us.

DIMENSIONS WALL VIEWED

To describe it to you...
Over and behind his head,
sits the electromagnetic spectrum
arrived and consulted.
Next it, the English monarchy
liberated from Windsor's abode
for a few pound.

There's Emerson's saying of virtue,
'That the one in most request, is conformity.
Self reliance as it's aversion
It loves not realities and creators,
but names and customs'.
Yet, you are forgiven!

Further on, there are the Northern Plains,
      a map of plenty!
      Said Dragon of Escher.
      Indian feathers and chime.
           The Chinese calligraphy for chaos.
           Poets, poetry and 'webcasting'.
           'Dragon Cloud' and calendar
and windows and hear-after.

'Ieee lad, 'tis fine to visit war with other men!
'tis fair, dincum and blue.
Not given because we deserved it...
given because we asked for it.
Ants asked for it.
Two Rino's that won't quit...
under-developed win and whit.
Under-developed from being over-developed.
And find swept-up circle and inclusion as twin.
And all time as in same swim.

AT HOME, MONDAY MORNING

Potential hazard - big dollar salary.
International assignments that wreck havoc
with personal life.
Following mammon everywhere.
Purchasing items that will be left as we leave…
For the short term, all to please.

Potential hazard - no gainful employment
of talents, of ideas, of what has been learned
and experienced.
Only sitting and waiting, watching for that last
chance to be really happy…
in our architecturally dispatched lodgings,
where these trappings speak volumes of us.

Potential hazard - lack of that sense of community,
lest it be Web browsing turned need,
as he seeds a patch of screen with said soil of his being.

If this, then all is not wanting what seems lost
to another time, that is past and has no current rhyme.
This *is* another time!

A tub of equilibrium.
A closet full of charms.
The last time they saw daddy,
He held them in his arms…
But now time moves at a great spiraling pace,
his closeness too far to be seen in this or in any place.

He wants to and is, there for you all.
His voice collapsing, as he drops through his fall…
It's on paper now 'cause it's easy, hard and sure?
No rebuttal, no consultation.
Only the voices y'all.

TENDENCY TOWARD HONESTY

He speaks of writing,
but won't do it every day,
because he's scared…
Maybe he'll do it every day!

Heavy metals descending in particles
about us.
So Dioxin comes from bleaching
white paper with chlorine - why?
I don't want that.
So dioxins come from burning/
using solvents - Dos words amigo, "Dry Cleaning"!
So dioxins are three hundred thousand times
more carcinogenic than DDT.
So dioxins come from burning plastics -
to clean up emission
Twiddle dumb and twiddle 'D'
And boy do we have plastics - needles in hospitality-less
hospitals.
Bottles of that, cartons of this
blissful obedience buy some more stuff!
Dioxin as big part of agents in orange.

Make no excuses for your strike at honesty.

In a bookstore today, saw again the face of
this difference.
This difference that stands too for white,
stands too for black.
Es Negro e blanko.
Es tu - fortuna de Dieu

THE DRAGON IS THE BAD GUY?

This too he cares not that you know.
He likes the story of St. George and has visited
England's St. George's Chapel at Windsor
and feels flesh and comfort in his liking odf\
that old place.

And more about dragons…
Ministers on television… preachers did say…
Comes the dragon, then the anti-Christ, the angel fallen!
What is this scrap.
I have a liking for the dragon symbolized,
dragon fought and respected nair well!
It does not mean that evil lurks unnecessarily
about what head and shoulders…
nor that I want to be like Mike
or any other foreign influence treating badly,
because all got was coming and brought on…
Well-traveled in it's attempts at mastery over we.

UNWINDING

Here luckily there is the feel of the floor.
Or is it simply that he's fairly sure he just walked in there.

A hint from the air that it is there.
He breathes,
no vacuum.

But, there are no people,
no sound, except the over-loud noise
made inside.
No chairs
no table
no smells if not smelling self
and this place has no light.

This place is here.
Where, eyes closed in a silent room, one is.
Where you think, feel.
Anywhere.
Safe.

SIMPLE

Pleasantly, have come through 'formal' education
relatively unscathed and somewhat better off.
Have learned what letters and sounds make-up this
or that word.
Have learned many years later, when not a chore,
to appreciate what reading brings.
To arithmetic and mathematics of the centuries?
Exposed and in some cases assimilated,
so not bitter there.

Civic studies and campus relations have given a base for
how to react to societal pressures, have taught the lessons of
diversity
and how to 'work' with people.
But truly,
schooling did not properly prepare,
for the unfolding moment now...collapsing.

INTERVIEW READ!...
....
Rd-t.t.p.-in.: ... "Shall we take a break?"
Rd-QS-in.: ... "No! Lets go on!"

COMPLETE

Your again
Seeing yourself firmly planted in
and coming up from
ground, earth, soil, sand and rock.
Grassy-knolls re-planted with signs that *plast* truth.
Not quite blast… which seems total irreconcilable.

Affected by it all.
Still in the look of an eye,
is seen 'that tunnel' -again- down which…spied…

KEEP IT ALL

Some have tended toward preserving what is old.
Others have tried at all costs to replace it with the new.
Hold your hands a shoulders width apart.
Now join them.

FEAR CHANGED

An out-world come in.
A left hand joined with a right.
White women with black men.
Oriental women with white men.
A black woman with every race of man to add 'that' strength.
Brown with red and the colors join and added to.
Even those not mentioned...not left out!

Edict delivered...
Women of that race here,
Men of that race there
Marry with your enemy,
Destroy the hate.
Marry with your opposite,
Enter in our fate.

We can save ourselves,
but only through a blending.
This, the long view indeed.
This view breaths easy as it looks out over millennia.

Mark these words...
There will be one,
but it will be composed of all.

Martin King's diversity.
"Individuals marry, not races!"

DARKNESS

And now, evening falls away.
Sun recedes behind horizon.
Forest on mountain is in slanted light.

Waning day yawns and slips below it's cover.
Night falls in with those dark influences that smear.
Stars all sing at once.

Creatures by the count wait to recite their parts,
to play upon the stage.
   Sorrow escapes.

Would a darkness to you, like my darkness'.
My darkness' are full of feel and knowing…
Knowings waited out.

Feelings given chance.
This arch-fullness is less for showing.
If could, would a softness to her softness',
would give you daily, pause for repair.

A good woman is more soothing than a bright morning.
A good nightfall in it's standard darkness, is mightier than all
swords.
An animal that trusts you, is a gift from the giver of gifts.

Sawn through on this mill for grist.
Dark new in an angry fist.
Black face, camouflage, war case.
Absent, not-seen, without light.
Darkness.

LESSONS PIECED TOGETHER

She is sustained by
her love of self,
as all life must do.

You and I are smarter than we think,
being common man.

Closed in on road below.
Through the blinds.
Closely touched.

Can not tell you of…falling down,
          the Blood of Thor,
          or office cure…
Awesome attribution is intended strange,
is dislodged. yeah! Arranged.

Back alleys
Black faces
Wild traces
Fertile valleys.

FOUR TIMES

Were he a Painter,
These scapes would have painted a long time ago.
But, being poet hearted fellow
have written of they, more than readers might like.

Washed ashore only yesterday
Lost as per latest course.
The trees do beckon!

It is less than ones city dwellings
for comforts, the trees…
But those too (comforts)
are largely of the mind.

Mendacity that tickles,
Stop when you aust
He says…ought and must
Scattered.

To sit back in chair or take the washing ashore
Either or.

Too, living at altitude
May be of main ingredient stature
When finally sifted through the organization
Running after you, luckily
Because you give no chase.

The man that from a woman runs is both sane and stupid.
An out for him, little exists.
A spout for her and him should untwist.
That helix is unravelable.

CHAUVINIST

Beast bellied
Tender parts sullied
Lost dying absent and home.
Warn of we outside.
In doors? Two moons

A bird chirping out window.
Twice third in the run from your eyes.
Nice outfit and rigging.
Splendid chaps worn and sod spoiled and ride.
Morrow for sunshine the bust-day is loose
dark washes and wastes
in your bright day, your sluice

He mines for the money
He mines for the challenge
He mines 'cause there's millions
right there near-by...malice

That whore is more valuable than near any other woman on
aerth!
Well, of course the question is why.
Because, if you'll entertain, she gives to a man, my my ...
She does not say no
because she too likes it, if at all possible.
And what an absolute blessing,
if nothing else!

WHAT IT IS

All writing is influence and distillation.
Be they poems, novels, songs, histories or such.
All truth enters, at once screaming and silent.
A man is a woman and a man.
A woman is a woman and a man.
The Earth is fragile and small.
"Archaeological evidence points to the possibility
of some African expeditions to the Americas from around
800 B.C."
And why not when all Earth's peoples trace their origins back to
that
Continent large.
And Vasco Nunez de Balboa reported in 1513 finding
a race of black-skinned people on the Isthmus of Darien in
Panama.
After destroying most of the Arawacks of Borinquen or Puerto
Rico,
Spain "introduced the first African slaves to take up the
workload"
in 1513 also.
"Native Americans and Africans and some Europeans met and
married
during these times and "a new people 'La Raza' was born".
"The pathfinders in Florida's interior were Africans
who fled the Carolina's…"
Names like the African Mandingo Francisco Menendez
who "fought the British for his people and the Spanish
and who finally settled on Spanish granted homesteads in
Cuba" are
remembered.
"A Spanish census of 1790 found that 18 percent of California's
colonists were Africans. They comprised 18 percent of the
populations
of San Francisco and Monterey, 24 percent of San Jose and
20 percent

of Santa Barbara."
Know this, my love.

Quotes from the scholarship of William Loren Katz and
others.

SOME

Of Wisdom, Alice Walker and others have said,
kindness is it's clear and clearest measure.
Buddhist and Hindu traditions are closer than most.
The man Jesus of Nazareth showed with his life
what a person should be...
always with truth, dignity, kindness.
Paul's work with Christianity shows enthusiasm
and caring.
What has happened since is everybody's guess.
Mohammad, may The Big Guy be with all prophets and saints,
was a man who wanted more for people.
More than dirt and filth and gods.
Buddha took it all in too.
All great men have great women around them.
All great women have great women around them.
See oh men! See what we hide from and scratch
about in the brush for,
on knees worn through, clear, to the other side.

This time and cloud passing...
What I will do, is go with you oh cloud!
Your journey mine!
Stated firmly, without apprehension,
yet a hint of, 'no I'd better not'!',
brought on by my alien-hand giver,
Self unrepeated.
Motorboat noisily sleeping,
a breath choke involved with feeling,
a series of breaststrokes, in water for bathing
and joyous afternoon mid-day scathing.

CONSTANCY

Circle unbroken, is every phenomenon.
I listen and listen still to you,
but what you say is what I say.
"Am sickened by my throwing away process."
So...when at a store, will, where can,
forgo the bag for instance.

We need us all to...
        This is where distinctions dissolve.
        Where sitting is the same as standing.
        Where I fly off un-attended and at once.
Panmixia...random matting
           in a population
           with no evidence of
           selection for traits.
More dictionary chatter, post-modernly given.

We need us all to...
Think of and see the world and us, ourselves, as no different.
This world and us as same.
There is much to the world, yes?
You mix.
You are one.
You meld.
Cloth, Rock, Plant, Plastic, Pharmaceuticals, Flesh, Air...
All same.

You are not hurt or lessened by your melding.
It is sometimes uneventful, this melding.
Sometimes 'staunch in its reception qualities'.
But always warm and alive.
There. Constant
See?

MORE ABOUT TRAVELING

Traveled far from secure home shores.
Waited out time insecure.

Then, with mouth,
Spoke blank verse consigned to rhyme.
Captured pure reason and common sense gave time.

Quiet and alone slept again in same bed.
Memories are scene set.
Sensing feathers in head.

Extended to length, wings can bring home
or flapping in libraries, can circle four moons.

Inside skull of all life abides,
that twinkle in eye,
that hole with no hollow,
that specific errantide.

PREVIOUSLY LEFT OUT

Dislike good movies that end.
As they end,
At their ending.
For being art bound with day,
would have it extend well into longer hours.
As with good music,
in mist
and midst of.

Bought an 1885 'ish copy
of Francis Bacon's Essay's
and hold the work some dear,
but not particularly the man.
Survival that leaves out 'surrival'
is not meat.
Machiavelli influenced again.
Yet, one incident can not define!

On subject of Father's and Mother's Day,
Once wrote, "would like to give my father
            the tops of farthest peaks,
            highest plateau over-looks
            and un-scripted means.
            My mother too.
            What church here.
            What vast scenery.
            What enduring needed needs.

SPIDERS IN BELFRY

Here, is my arachnid heaven!
Home for them, home for me.
Windshield,
screen door, wall.
As for me!
Bed, refrigerator,
door and escape.
Room for all buddy.
Whiplash, wake.
Here all is the mountain.
Mountain orders all.
Weather, climate, control and waif
Palm-busted, river-rusted through-see and gate.
Ah! *&%$# it! It waste time and tough
Frontward to backford, only slight-need and must.

DIALOGUE

Got television in the back drop,
A headache from smoking two cigarettes today
And two far strewn holdings inside yesterday's lost
musings,
Layered in antipathy with acrimony wandering around in
fore-ground.

Lately you approach even closer to your loss in winning!
Pictures speak back from wall,
with signatures given by riders that would,
and fathers that ought.
As motorcycle was purchased today.

Paltry seclusion, backyard intrusion,
yellow angry and trust,
Upsidedown outside untouched.

Labour weasing as I desire to tell a story.
To weave into yon tale
and bring home for viewing,
a standard meaning that had in it's revealing,
real truth for it's telling.

Warned you of allowing others to speak too highly of you.
Of getting yourself in that fix.
But that light sought
is bitingly found, with the upsidedown move
that signals corruption un-bound.

All men for selves.
Women trust in shelves.
Wellstone from Minnesota,
Democrat, spoke like man enraged with his conviction that day.
It was a Sunday.
A sunny July day.

What I find for self, for contemplation,
is desire to help the dis-enfranchised of every type and shoot.
And no-reaction is unsecured in wallow
where hide'eth I.
Not to loose control, not to give experience too much voice.

NO MORE

I'll tell you what I don't like.
I don't like how callous we are,
Not can be, are.

How with a little outside influence in unpopular directions
people of some power…police, etc.,
riot gear themselves and the wasted
into an oblivion that has all of man's history,
as excuse and hidden, then open, then closed again meaning.

Of value so small is sticking out one's chest,
that to do it, at all, is a waste.
And lives that will last many decades ahead
have this day lost an innocence,
through structured violence, Ok'd by 'adults',
that can hardly be achieved again.
The Irish of every stripe teach their kids to hate.
The Bosnian, the Namibian, the Pakistani,
the Black Muslim and White Power 'klans.
There are so many, that naming has to be representative and stop
here.

LIFE ON OUR TERMS

If next *life* is to be granted, it must be *taken* inside of that,
God too, will not suffer fools.
And bringing Euripides forward/backward, to *modern*
thought,
'Goodness and being in (God) are one. He who imputes ill
to
(Him)
makes (Him) none.'
So, you cannot skip and wave and dance your way through.
Appled seed and tackled need, it will be easy and hard to
do.

BEYOND THE LAST

I dare say, poetry is not nor are, some soft stuff.
There are those who in their heeded calling,
have gathered do gather life, while distilling and telling,
what life would have gathered, distilled and (I will) telling.

Many mistakes made and captured before they blew off in a
wind.
Brahms, because he plays in the background,
is stronger than I.
Those 'Hungarian Dances'.
Ah! Repetition, as I promised.

And if I cough up previous things said in a telling,
bare me only the harm applicable to a lost soul, needing.
Then all else of your inputs will be of the plus sign
and gear-altered to subject mortification to our chore perceived
and narrowly accepted.
That of, 'you do not exist'.

A handy bifocaled look down the dragons third throat
as I pass passing.
As my imagination welcomes me past the last lasting.

HEALTH

Think,
I may be bitter...
About children...mine
About habits...mine
About thoughts...mine.

Apologize, for taking up view.
For getting in line of sight.
Heated political (boy! Don't like using that word)
races running wild.

What dignity?
What history?
Where unthawed truth.
Whence working solutions.
...Not called such,
because it has little art to it...
Won't say none.

Health is...
Your self-inflicted pain achieved
via knowing exercises,
done daily, etc.

STARTED OUT TO APOLOGIZE

Gadfly? Maybe!
Do seem to teach out pedanting.
Play in there, in kiddy area,
until can come out as innocent.
Backing up again, toward goal.
Coming in sideways,
Dropping from chair.

Growing from the ground
Coming up.
Bouncing off walls.
Climbing on the chest.
Gaining little of value, save relationships,
agony and fun.

When through?
When enough over-much?
Throw tigers back to mounted earth.
Let all who climb to heights to sit,
cramp necks for more of same.
Let all who grow to love medicine
walk those trails.
Let bums be bums and matadors stay home.
Let bulls walk you out back with two bull guards.
Take charge of liking!
Like people, atmosphere, oxygen, like hydrogen,
like helium…since above all these you are.

Like water and sky, like
Soil and rock and barren ground wait
to have you finally come close enough to see…and be awed.
To then be so thankful, that now finally all lost is found.
Quiet can envelope again inside any standing reality.
Like metal and mettle. Have both in like form.
Hone skills of an anteater. Travel home.

STILL!

He is surgical in his dealings with people, but not unkind.
>He is indulgent and bearing and propped up by 'other' forces too.

Yeah! You *should* abandon this warrior speak and translation.
>Because what it bears is costly to much mixing with people,
>save during work hours.

Which then means that when you read an hour earlier what Emerson said
>of Boneparte, both good and bad, and when you took it as a good sign,

a knowing, understanding me finally. Yeah! We are together in this joining, I felt
>That way too, even before you said it kinship...

What say you now after being upbraided greatly by the woman
>about this warrior mindset.

Methinks I can clearly see her female side.
>The only thing men do in battle, is die.

Die now, die later.
>Die of this, die of the other.

So then it is your own each, to live as you see it is.
>If 'they' attack, and you must fight to live, then die trying.

If you are being protected from harm by the body of that man,
>then think not the mind so singular.

TO PESSIMISTIC HEIGHTS

A scene.
Men in battle will take riches, money,
and women.
All treasures.

They kill and maim
not without a little apprehension.
'Tis awful work.
As described, as demanded
as proscribed, as commanded.

Fighters, support staff, messanger
and cook alike.
All and more enter and leave scene
coming and going on this board of a bard.
Aren't there other stories could be told.
Is there no good side to man's history.
No. Not while anthrope war is part.

SPOUSAL ABUSE

Were I not one who writes,
inspired by, repulsed by the world,
I would be an angel.
A protector of this world and all worlds,
that crop up out of natures chaotic work.
The beauty is often too difficult
and embarrassing to look at.
Married to this Aerth
           the

NOT TO DISSEMBLE

Entertainment, like the falling away of peel from orange,
reminds us of our insides.
There is joy, laughter, wonder, sadness, surprise.
It tallies up our extravagances and remarks our loathing.

Readings in which one encounters a like mind, as set down
recently or
many years before are private bullion's, personal strikes,
much
precious metal found.

Why some writers, those who seek unabashedly for their
truths, often
say all that can be said, in one sentence, is a miracle.
Then so many sentences and onward and astonishment and
smiles from
the reader.
It becomes a series of reinforcements *and* a re-tooling of the
entire shop floor
all together and at once.
And always is there learning.

This is why libraries are built and stocked,
why universities and schools had to be peopled.
Because a few or many good minds thought aloud,
guided us while seeking their way.

And debt is strong, secured.
Task is right interpretation.
Not to read and hide because you disagree,
not to dissemble.

Knowledge given by the writer and facts, should not be
lost,
because of wish to keep people down and at call.

The world is largely built now by our labors, in fact, over-
built, so…
Mexican History can be taught, in truth.
African and Black History can be taught without fear.
Often unwritten but spoken Indian History, all Indians, all
natives can be revealed.
And everything concerning accomplishments and achievements
of women through the ages can be safely uncovered,
thrown up
on the screen in full view of all.

In all of this, minds unite as one humanity, saving this
planet and others
from harm.

NATIVE THANKS

Moon 34 walked across stage yesterday.
Sunny2, not revealed.
Password way to oblivion.
Through this, time is squeezed out of squinted looking.
Monsters walk through sleep, remembering youth.

Today, during night and morning, such dreams were dreamt,
that beat-out any amusement or thrill every had.
Non obtrusive, all welcomed soon upon presentation.

Waking at 3:30 a.m., alarm was turned-off.
Waking again at 6:30, boss was called.
And at 10:30, thought it meat,
I should join the waking day.
Spirit feather, this Dream Catcher seemed turned full on.
Thank you!

POLES AND WHAT'S BETWEEN

Writing when tired produces what?
Misspelled words?
Or topsy-turvy world viewed right side up finally?

Think more than anything, sight is lost
while many sightings are recorded.
And things that should be seen by all are
covered in the usual mis-trust, dust and toil,
which should have been welcomed as friend,
instead of watched like criminal.

To capture all the good is same as lounging with a Zeus.
To welcome our ghosts is to re-sift the narrow sluice.
A god is weathered by our constancy of mistake.
Shod, consider self ridden through long bright night leaving
no trace.

Life is eloquent in right tidy hands.
Left to liar, mistakes all right demands.
'Amble on up to sign-post ahead distant'
Be on right-guard for laughter and treason.
All alike, you will take part
a view with the clouds
a far below ground listing.

JUSTICE II?

Quoting King.
Once, killing King
Following King
Running up Kings exposed back and frontside.
Yeah! The government mine, yours and…
Who's in charge?

Where's the guy who got the equipment here,
Hoisted or walked it in the building?
Made sure it got strapped.
Took the hours, the cost.
Estimates a working plant soon.
Gathers William Brennanesque Justice gone a short time
ago.

So close, all the great men and women within arms length
literally.
Who dying now leave legacies greater than even our
precious mountains
       and loved forests. What Virgin ground and life
       around.
              What forties/fifties, eighties/nineties.
       Every slap on this telephone back,
       Rushes onward to our cooling
       and never lost to our wandering aimlessly
       let us push and chase injustice with a kind-
       justice.

BAD SEED

Change of venue many indeed be in order.
If there's time, off to Montreal, then to Paris.
There to uncover selves inside a self.
Or there to follow countless others to some fine oblivion.

Charge all misgivings with the high treason.
Alter destinies in every way your pleasin', choice makin'
parts suggest.
Run hapless and helpless into the foreign wind.
Ask firmly what drives you is safe.

Safe, all the lives that depend on.
Safe, the countless worlds at two of Time's poles,
Past and Future.
Safe, how wide the embrace.
Safe the closen space.

Why must any person who wishes otherwise do what you
suggest,
Any you!

BLADE AND MAKER BRIEF

Cuts well!
Its thatch and reed make beautiful mats,
indoors and out.
Bamboo is of great importance to
Panda, scaffold and cutting.

Use of lemon tree wood
gave maker cause for alarm,
but...so many stories
of the work these blades have done,
that no real surprise is had.

Sing sword-makers praises.
A willing blade handed over to one deserving?
Respect of not breathing on it.
Expected cleaning after use.
Ceremony, chore.
Proper holding.

Walked toward the coming Way.
Ancient Way of Sword.
Sought out your acceptance and lessons.
Never faultered in delivery.

After floors were scrubed by scrubs.
After warm-ups, seiza...
long after Aikido's kata's, throwing and holds,
came Battodo, more sweat and still wonderful Tameshigiri.

Power controlled and had.
Camaraderie, tea and saki.
The adulthood, the childhood, the watch me
and see uses not yet weathered
by the long blades seasons.

IN PURSUIT

Game face on now.
Spy the wrinkles.
Watch the shrivel and the gray.
Get shorter by quarter inches.

Here it is.
Throw off habit of wanting, as much as can.

All writers must fear as they write.
If only out of one's past experiences
or from knowing throughout history,
writers, men and women, have suffered so.
Have lost life and limb in pursuit of task;
To write after a recounting.
Some near-fire watching.
No lap-dog had.

Ah! Let pen walk under cover of hand.
Welcome mind to wallow in sand-trap miseries
Help self to momentum's strapped to ship leaving just now,
headed beyond these shores.
Then wake from secret sleep
And come into bright night of day.

SELF ADHESIVE

Wampum and shop'um
Father, gather at the surface moon feasted.
Willing never to whey-strewn existence on
broken shoulder of jutting-earth-meet sea shore soon.

Sit here of a Saturday and do this?
To what end.
With what means.
Questions asked after a Szymborska-ing.
Of no punctuation for questions.

Simply a twisted-sister, with all due Respect.
And to be twisted of a windy smoky early August morn'um.
Is to be welcomed into sanct'um of the evil-twist in nature.

Wind whips around because it does
and can.
Trees balance themselves for the blowing
and sometimes fair's fair is none.
Oh! To follow all bards.
Look there! There's a scathing going on!

GLIMPSING EQUANIMITY

Leaf captured as it fell into hand.
Phrase found on tip of pen.
Sound of doors closing across glen.
Of dog bark, of coyote yell.

Bear come under cover of night.
Big cats seen tiptoeing up shear cliff sides.
All that comes is going.
And black earth and star burst equally reside.

Home is blue globe.
Our water hung in this air.
My dirt between these toes.
And sunlight and none both watched carefully there.

Now, of companions welcomed before leaving.
Of family taught how my breathing
Does stay my steady hand and wreck my social bed.
How wind feels on face and in hair,
Of common place and blessed fair.

Of insect flight that traverses known cures.
Of selfish love, of pride, of enrapture.

All belong twice three times and one.
Part with six of thirteen and shunned.
Where witches practice light arts miscued.
Miscued of purpose, darkside reused.

Awakened all, that parts of life tried.
Clasp hands in hall or totally outside.
Stand under pillars fashioned straight from earth's trees.
Or sit by quietly, ours too, all of these.

ONLY A MAN

In the last few days, exercised a hard living.
Put to writing a few 'tales told'.
Searched about for handhold on company laptop
that a summer-hire loaded new software on…
Head shaker that.

Watched many a movie. Eaten well.
Thought of her, pined for her.
Stayed just this side of her, a little out of view.
Detachment worked.

Why you ask.
Yes! Well it's sure.
The world though large
encapsulates we.
And a smallness that shows all is spied.

And showing all to lookers for same
is just the thing one ought not do.
But no sacrifice, no gain!
What now would you have, more fame?
And then a fine austerity westward-hoo's itself
straight away.
And there, presently before you, shot down those tunnels,
an eye meets an eye…
More fairy tales unfold.

Would that *my* world be big and blue
with brown, red, yellow, black and white.
With arguments, whispers and jars a-opening.
As led by the dialogue and silenced by sure.

ASK ONE WHO KNOWS

Scare tactics practiced daily.
Utilities reigned in.
Warnings of new tax liabilities.
Whole societies closed down.

Obtuse angles turned acute.
Circles revealed of their straight lines.
Cubes taken from cylinders.
And round pegs into holes.

As we fetch our way along the journey,
pink bathrooms and innocence are remembered from our
youth.
Sink baskets top-down on far side of any court kept
crowned.

Shear invention in twilight of wordy phrases.
Thought a retard 'cause of lost wages.
But what is bought with pieces of soul,
had better be worth it.
Had better re-turf it and bury all allowance
in well-depth of inter-ground co-mingling.
For resealing at other times single-ing.

A TRANSLATION

"Several stories about regular folk."
Fine verse for television, in context.

The way he says it or she or I,
Does not cancel wanting all.
Wanting each to say it. Say that we are one.
Have sung songs with groups of men
and in that camaraderie saw every warlike gathering.
All the take the gold, climb to the top, we against them.
False building.

Cross several finish lines of one's own, daily, if must.
When men meet there is a taking from and a giving up.
All by force.
Force of Will, force of means.
Always a force of threat, touche',
Tout a fait, tout de suite,
tout ensemble, tout le monde.

REMINISENCE AS VEHICLE

Found lots odf Obata Sensei stuff on Web today, did I.
Try fly high, picture self seen there.
Always too many people.

Always my own way too.
Sure and there can be little doubt,
that we gave of ourselves, of a practice.
And yeah! We took much.
And still do any who with backward dance slide
down channel not so wide, to make the day as told,
Can walk away with gold made new and worthless, next
truth of one.

Not one as in just you.
One in as much you.

WRESTLING

The diamond cutter
And the dragon sleeper.
Goldberg, Rock of faith.
WCW, NWO et on.
et on.

WHAT UP?
(A TRIBUTE)

The blessings are far more than can be seen
in hundreds that can be seen in an instant.
A realization instant.
Coming under influence thankfully.
And what is always climps'd,
Is the connectedness of all phenomena and things.

When serious, all run.
When blues, run they, then come.
When gospel, cometh they.
When tribal, most hide, all come.
When Coltrane...
When rap...

> Anger is just below skin and over horizon,
> encompasses all, because I say so!
> We the people!
> 'Downed by a peace treaty'
> 'Straight out 'a Compton!'

75

PART OF WHY

They know what they do as they seem to throw
relationships away.
Sign and seal a lonely fate.

Mostly unforgiving, yet wishing forgiveness,
they work at leaving a legacy of thoughts, of observations,
from their lowly height.

NOT YOUR OWN

Don't want to come back later.
Won't sleep under stair.
>No tapestry on walls thirty feet high.
>No Labour losing in game four-times taken.

But watch it, we're 'coming up from down'.
We're type-set all around.
We've welcomed all and ground swell,
Of momentum set-back in mold-hell.

>Into third time, to stop this is thought.
>Well-healed in snack-field after groceries I bought.
>And onward to horizon seen backward through
>mirror,
>'In rooms' and 'out rooms' and 'out rooms' are best...

>Though, 'in rooms' talk of Monroe Library in
>Fredericksburg
>And Jefferson et al.
>Talk of integrity and truths hurled in the air.

>Some slavery, some shown-as-same,
>Four-fifths of awful, three-fifths of guilt-name.
>Line-up all ye tending, we're one seventy-five
>today.
>This message is trapped 'neath your tender
>unspoken.
>Outsourced to Indiana, snail-remembered, a token.

ONE LEFT

You must strive at it.
The striving (to belabour) is all.
The long walk back or there.
Time spent away from.
Tirade had in head far inside.
By-way steeped, instead of highway so wide.

What small towns lost to some foreign investor.
Where forest that was there before.
Sold to whom? Why they cut there's down
centuries before, now they come for ours!
I find that obscene.
And cause for obscene alarum may be given yet!

Am back, no skipping around with some jutting eyes.
Surprises once so, are no more.

Perhaps you would have it, I "straighten up and fly right".
Maybe "bebop daddy, don't you blow your top." is sacred
verse.
Lean over here with me now… what of visitors from
'elsewhere'.
Are we soft, comfortable humans in anyway sanguine of
our chances, under an unforeseen all-powerful threat?

'They have no men there!'. No practitioners!
Ah wait! There may be some.
What here comes walking, what hero stamp this?
Where rough comparisons now?
This one may do.
And what sir is your name.

MORE ON WRITING II

To sit consciously to write
What had little form before,
Is a wish, an estimate, something
Describing what is to come.
And surely a best guess.

So, you do it anyway.
Whatever the weather.
Still behind shaded screen you
let fingers dance, mind trot and whit's wit.
If, any of those can be said to reside there.

And so also, it would be nice to hear others speak
openly and truthfully about your work
and find most happy there.
Having let yourself think thought-less thoughts,
        Those shaded in the glow of ones always thought.
This truly is goal.
This what may elude,
but what must be tried.
This your chance, your shot, your work.
Fashioned it is hoped, of a spacious resolution.
To help more than to help.

THE HERMIT WOULD AGAIN SPEAK

Out the back way, out.
Through the trap door shut.
Mark your third row thus,
Plant your Polly Hill experiments.
On your vineyard Martha.

And I should say that Osgood did it to me again.
Had me waiting the morning, the vibrant Sunday Morning.
…Spent time studying Bakersfield personals yester-morn.
Admit it here as a test of how torn.

Stein-Row cubicles written twice on the wall,
Market forces wrangle, while paparazzi follow…
Some angle, some straight-back, some wiggle, some pawn.
Oblong extensions, extruded through no yawn.

The world-at-large may have lost it's heart this day.
Lost a princess, who wiped her hands of few things and
people,
Lost a helper, a wand, a hand of the Hand, a mother.

Lost two in the battle to wake up the heart,
But, I'm costing quite a few left to take-up the start.

Amble indeed, on up the road ahead distant.
Stamp 'staple' on your wrapping from learning and fable.
Your wrapping you wrap after genes and tight-twisting.
Each tapping well craved, leaves one washed in drum-
beating.
The heart beating in the mind,
The want of yesterday, more time.
The grab it back in
Letters written thin.
Calls made after whim and fancy,
No order, little pre-thought, few to Margaret, none to Nancy.

BLEST

Tapped sorrow.
Sapped morrow.
And marrow caught between.

Flat charred in a yard-based shards appeal.
Microphone spoken, face shown a pokin'.

Conducting business as usual and base.
Seducing she-earth with deception and censure.
Found in graveyard with your tongue in your ear.
Skipping sidewalks for fauna trailed paths over here.

So, lets try this.
For me, it is the sound of the words.
Lately I think, I am honored to know/hear certain words,
names,
Ideas too leave me blank and blest.

No politician, nor anyone should bait the other countries
in this wide world with talk like 'we are blessed by God'.
(When we in fact take precious resources from these others
for our ease and wealth.)
Because we are all blessed by Him.
Yeah! We have cleaner water in some instances,
Sometimes cleaner air, better regulations against stupidity
on occasion,
But all blest by God.

AN UNWISE HUNTER

Stow crows feet ambivalence 'neath dresser so wide
Late show trusted in a back seat little slow,
Honor upright and cleanly-miss, sligh Bullseye's, slight
part.

Contorted we twist into our savior-gross start.
Spitting around below on a spitter of a bike.
Come closer, intolerant now I'll bust you a cart.

Little wheel-ride a coming
little skin-hiding a going.
Little hike plied a knowing,
Like Actaeon, over-extended and loving...
It waddled, toe-roping, closer to it's closing.

SHAKESPEARE AS CATALYST

.."speak to me as to thy thinkings,
As thou dost ruminate, and give thy worst of thoughts,
The worst of words.   "Taken alone these words speak of an
honest mind.
But here too, honesty is not enough!
With them, the unpitiable Othello barks instruction to the
Lying dog *friend* of all basic minds, Iago.

Being a dark man, I'll not make over-much of this telling,
But some trifles come to mind.
Is not this, as are all Shakespeare's tragedies, tragic.
Is it not true that men will slip about under cover of night
Or any advantage gleaned, to snare and entrap after their
own
Falsity and longing?

Have cared for white woman on more than one occasion.
Has been a function of my upbringing and varied blood,
that
An attraction to all fine women has been at my side as
flowers
To good soil.
In this attraction of opposites, one has accepted a known truth.
A truth at once silent and loud.
A truth subdued by the same unholy hosts, that would kill
exact history
To attend their stolen wealth's.

Dissemble at eventual peril.
Teach overall, unwarranted fear and loathing with fear
showing.
Truth of what is happening and what has happened.
Is similar to effect of sun and moon on sea and waterway.
Truth like water from earth rises where it can be seen as
cloud,

Then falls back to earth, to begin task anew.
There is no complete hiding.
Revelation *is* nature.

An Emilia, a Cassio, any who seek and see character not
difference only, are wise.
But a fool was never made that was not a fool in love.
Be they man or woman.
And this *love* is stinging and stinking and strung through
with misery.
It will let neither rest, but calluses all.
Yet, without it, we must discover a stronger word than
peril,
To describe our blighted, sad condition.
Hence, this too is accepted as man's fate, "No way but this -
Killing my self to die upon a kiss."

THEN

Worst thing a man can do is kill a woman or child.
Then the worst are the larger environment, that contains
Mole, insect, animal and mammal you.

Bird and spare reptilian source Othellian, we're rebellion'
Water sore-bitten and Todd sure coming-iin'.
One could be mad about a great so many things.
And that begets a place where all that can be presented is
and that is a bit too much and far to near not enough,
that if shadows wish to dance across my space and wall,
it is quite enough and more so a tall order answered.

Come in all, welcome.
It is I the one who cares not.
On no! Not the one who cares not.
This avoided of all was told us as child
This above all is rank and wild.
Not bad, 'cause bad it can not be.
Flee free his fie fee anger, his fits-field, his free.
Its you me and we.

DRAGON

Told to sit in a corner
All fairytales are goners
Hands clenched, fingers locked
Fly way through the air 'cause
He threw ya.
Spy angle midway and see tuna
And through ya.
Deep of water and air.

You know, it comes home to him now and again,
What an absolute block-head he might have stayed,
Had he tried hard and prayed…on
Through watched millennia down any of the three throats,
Of dragon so wide.

Didn't want to speak of him again.
He Dragon.
He spare none, in quest, to see, to try be,
A man no, a man yes.
In ceremony with this other.

HE - OVERMAN

Jewels thrown against rock walls,
Always told how to behave.
Altitude, a flying dude.
Oh boy! You'd *better* look over your shoulder!
You'd better watch your'n and others soft back.
'Cause from this angle cowards attack.
Though 'tis sure to him, 'tis in the winning.
To you, you must add sinning
And meaning where there is little.

This makes you a philosopher or a catholic,
but don't pin 'those' badges ('we don't need no...") on your
vest.
Only want to see everyone happy, healthy and wise.
Wise is not the last one here, wise is the first with the
healthy.
Want none to hurt, and it is so...
Want good for you and mostly it is done.
Want miles from Earth, then watch it run.

Now! Do you think that a good man must be good.
He this one, can do other, because he is not other.
The idea of the over-man...frightening to women and
children,
To men, something to be tamed
Or a combatant foresoothed and ta'en.
A poor cooth uprisen and sprayin'.

STORIES TOLD

Come close again. Let these whispers catch your ear.
Will tell of how once when hate was remote,
when differences perceived, were not.
When all the little children played and laughed
and did learning together...
All tasted life as one and part.

In this place parents went to work yes!
But these same parents did not neglect themselves, their
families,
Nor the larger neighborhood, when fortunate to have same.
And corporations understood,
Got if finally.

In this place Indian names and places were called such
always out of reverence and mounting awe.

Africans that gave their blood, toil and reason to the soil,
European father who would catch-up your mother
And beat down your father, now you (and build some more
sh'*+),
was not forgotten.

In this place great art takes place.
Great whit slips one hundred under your hotel-room door.
Many writers and thinkers of before, are hoisted still, above
our heads.
Still are paraded through the 'every street' and 'back alley'.
Still are seen as icons to our story. And should!

Let no more, the bustling three-(wring it out 'a ya) circus of
success,
failure and prejudice,
wipe the dirty, dis-used bathroom floor of every scaly,
disjointed,

ugly wiping monster, with your front and side-ways face.

Let us actually make it home after having traduced your gauntlets a-many.
All the group speak aplenty.
This, the story would have told.

A 'story', yes and how sad…
But, we must interrupt. Never was a story told, that did not contain
sanctioned portions of the actual inspiration for the tale.
So jump over building and help tired earth,
Let mind meet fantasy on realities fine, fluffy turf.

SHARING

'Narrow escapes' based forwarding schemes.
Feral pets jumping whole rescue teams.
Spying much for learning extant in the world.
Climb high in the clouds 'neath your airy sky home.

Attention *not quiet*, to you do we speak.
Distended guts ripe with the watering by liquids.
Sat down on one hard one 'cause your female and willing.
Amalgams do visit us not nil.

Obliged once, to capture a wife.
Now scared twice and three times for sure.
Feet flat on floor as you type.
Back arched straight, chin pointing within.

Hand across chest.
Chores awaiting our best.
Last battling the air with two weights many morns.
Coming away enthused, better limbered,
Stronger of 'head and shoulders', but less charming.

A full cities tour, a backyard junket.
Two bellies fomenting disjunctive's and tooling-up
For the, it seems wanted, heralded as coming,
Last-days Armageddon wars.

But, know you, of discussions had often near top of hill.
Where it is rediscovered daily, that extended, strenuous
effort
is good for and improves at equal paces,
our growth, strength and duration, maybe.

Tolerance devises sewn into every living head.
Wages thrown in a wee pit with management's salary and
bonuses.

A camp-fire, a horse-ride, the wilderness I said.
Portions equaled to nothing…to something instead.

MY CITY

Baby yeah!
Way up in a corner.
Blest still and always to see out these eyes.
Blest for having seen a bobcat in the wild,
Eagle on the wind, condor on wing.
California gives it all. Los Angeles in thrall of major foreign undulation.
Los Angeles being San Diego and Bakersfield included.
Out to Bishop, but not beyond. One long finger to Phoenix.
Out on the water even, pictured Pacific welcomed storms.
Drive quickly to Oxnard and Ventura, midway to Santa Barbara its over.
All big cities throughout our world hold their own,
'Reach tentacles' spread winds directions.

Don't give a sh..for impressing you.
Your boredom you must manage.
Sixth passage spoken opens door over rail.
Dash through in hurry or moon-lost on this trail.
Black holes open up soon, voyage short.
You entered leaving and your comeback's taboo.
Now you can sit in a villa in Spain,
Drink tea in the twilight,
Remember your rain.
Rain you owned with the ownership of that place.
Stains delivered to pavement on ancient American soils.
Now away from, you moan their being elsewhere
And wish you were 'home'.

At home see pictures of St. Petersburg in head,
Of Veronezh and the road to *and* Lipetsk.
Of the women seen there in Russia so fair.
Of pride of spine, of discipline air.
And holding and reviewing on occasion the journal you did keep,

See the stress, the trial of the trip in the hard press of the
pen,
In the swath and sway of ten thousand armed men and
women in a minute.
But mostly in land old and bursting new.

Of Paris…a day can be more than enough,
To catch you brokering your eyes from the glare, the good-
glitter, the stare.
There's Kalispell and Cheyenne, Whitehorse, Smithers and
Anchorage,
Amsterdam, London, Keller and Frazier, New Orleans,
Montreal, Atascadero.
Try any Paris Bridge, that's all.

BEST TO STAY THERE AND WRITE

Distinct from him is every fun loving man.
He's taken it from his pockets and thrown it disdainfully to
the sand.
Best he stay there and write!
A mangled entry in a shepherds brown book,
Tangled bat wings in soup, with eighth volunteer cook.

When a melancholy like syrup pours over,
Take it, you're there with more than a few.
Best you stay there and write!
We march the distance thought too far to make.
Seen on the road, with our bowl, our plate.

One thing needed to round out this life.
Woman who's whore, friend and wife.
Best you stay there and write!
Looking for much in this life of grief.
Tomorrow to be poet, mate, maybe a chief.

No lessons, no teachings, stay clear of the breach.
Walking 'round the backside takes a few years to reach.
Best you stay there and write!
Rhyme simply with extensions to pain.
Out with this anguish, away with vain attempts to explain.

A vacation at home, a week in the hay.
He'll run, he'll walk, he'll bear-crawl away.
He'll sit there and write!
Some Aikido in the morning's, late at night.
This physical body knows exactly what's right.

Transfixed to a winning like tar on a road.
Up comes it's parts showing, a little kiss for this toad?
Best you stay there and write!
Look deep in the night.

HOW DRAGON EARNS WHAT STATUS

A growl, nay a roar, too few sanctified chores.
Too little screaming into the wind and at night.
Not a lot of stepping to the plate.
Pitches come quite fast oh yes!
Speeches made at bay and rest.

Sat-by quietly as you scampered over the crowd with your
easy manner.
All impressed, even I.
Now I fly by a fly-by.
One more soar on these wings will land me firmly on your
cap.
Not what you want, be you any mate or chap.

John 'Trane would not let-up shouting those strains in a
willing ear.
Dolphy to the rescue, nothing usual there.
We waited for Tom Waits long enough back then,
Welcome wanted friend.

All came at their right time
to inspect and hire-out our learning and right awe.
Have had my Compton boom-box streets,
London chauffeurs,
Several hard hawg-rides North, a number South, East, a
little West.
In the saddle over the rise.
Always an ample, willing rough-test.

Had a buddy once, whom I took to be a hard man...never a
tear in the eye,
No remorse, nothing done wrong, even if so.
A natural soldier, a warrior, sports hero, one also self-
contained
          Practiced our manhood's.

Took nothing for granted.
Study the classics.
Find out about Africa's silent history.
Lift weights, be they bought Iron or axles in the dust.
One to walk over the horizon with, his back yours, your
back his.
One to walk into battle with or ride abreast with on wings
of some huge birds
Just found and tamed for the purpose some days before.
My point in this start-up, is to say that he said to me one
day,
After drinking a little smoke and smoking a little drink and
hard blow
assignments to our torso's each, that I was a hard man.
Well I take it as an honour, as a badge (we still, don't need
no stinking…).
Practice on!

FACES

AT

REST

II

...#.LOG READ! ...Signal-in.:

…………………………………..

…………………………………..
…………………………………..

INTERVIEW READ!...

……………………………….
Rd-QS-in.: … "Looking back in your own history…"

In Pangaea the super continent of 175 million years ago,
Gondwanaland was center maybe!

"So good men will not consent to govern for cash or
honours. They do not want to be called mercenary for
exacting a cash payment for the work of government,
or thieves for making money on the side; and they
will not work for honours, for they aren't ambitious.
We must therefore bring compulsion to bear and punish
them if they refuse - perhaps that's why it's commonly
considered improper to accept authority except with
reluctance
or under pressure; and the worst penalty for refusal is to be
governed by someone worse
then themselves. That is what, I believe, frightens honest men
into accepting power, and
they approach it not as if it were something desirable out of
which
they were going to do well, but as if it were something
unavoidable, which they cannot find anyone better or equally
qualified to undertake. For in
a city of good men there might well be as much competition to
avoid power as there now
is to get it, and it would be quite clear that the true ruler
pursues his
subjects' (electorate's) interest and not his own;
consequently all wise men would prefer the benefit of this
service at the hands of others rather than the labour of

affording it to others themselves."

-Socrates   Via   Aspasia, Plato
and others

POPEYE OMAHA

I wear it all
On the outside!
Mistrust.
Disappointment.
A telling frost.
Tepid noose.
Sorry we came!
Goodby 'till we meet again!
Don't stand there!
Don't look there!

I will,
        stand there
        look there.

We are one universekind
I like what I like
And 'I wam what I wam!'

Allowed to make no living,
Therein little chance for;
Fancy soaps.
Lounge clothing.
Perfumes.
coiffure.
And then to hate so.
It is truly human folly.
It is a bad living.
A dead beacon.
        A turned-out light.
        redundant overture.
        unkempt thought.
        dirty spook!

A HAUNTING

A woman's abandon is not just 'a' thing.
It may be the 'only' thing.
As may be yours to her.

received, 'bell, book and candle' rites,
Before ready.
There was more rot to do.
But now, wreck havoc and die young.
Walk a merciful path and strum strings of lyre.

With high dudgeon all was given up to you,
As one walks through mire of losing a family,
Of bluesing a lost thing.

Pictured as you are now in minds eye borrowed.
Float across room in gown and Sassoon.
Toast fine life, in track, tune.

Houses in which one lived, seemed to haunt only themselves.
No boast.
The creak and crack of walls, footsteps hidden across halls.

If you should haunt, it might as well be me!
For I am match!
In this wretched state you are sought, for the challenge.
In this oneness cultivated? Left open yet well closed.

Some part of me would have you perceive me as a sad man,
But know me…
As a bad man doing good under extreme duress
And good argument.

PHYSYCOPHASIA

Ya gotcha, sober transitions.
Yer, somber translations.
Si' temples are crying!
Of, vwe disdain.
May we?

Physycophasia.

THIS SATURDAY & SUNDAY
(MORE CATALYST)

Time slipped in the snow and fell for a while here, this
morning.
First snow.
Autumn at height is winter.
But winter at height is just hard...
And beautiful.
Only a few miles up from here, deep winter.

We find him hearing-back some tapes also,
Placing Tom Waits in the mix...
Strongly coming.

And of course, Nusrat Fateh Ali Kahn is homeboy.

Thinking then of music made by us as mid-eighties
Played into late nineties and here now.
How work stranded us. Lost!

Had a Sunday walk today. Took a volume of African
history.
Went out half an hour from the house.
Through neighborhood into mountains,
Up into more pine forest, where after checking for wildlife
Disturbed by my nearness, read for a spell,
Hiked down to lower ground and found a trail
Ripe for 'bear-crawls', which are more like bear-runs...
On all fours, remember football training.

A few dogs were disturbed by this walk.
One of which seems to belong to the house
Where three young women stretch and turn themselves
In the sun ("mine eyes have seen the glory...").
Female form...oh blessed work!
Face, hair, eyes, neck.

Shoulders, arms, hands and breast.
Belly like the Sahara herself, warm soft and calling.
Below this latitude...all heaven breaks loose.
I stand Falling!

THE THING AND ITS CONSEQUENCES

Triple by-pass pussies, for this guy without a woman so
long.
Look, I want women who love to sit, clean with their legs
wide open.
>These, examples of things ought *not* be said.
>Traveled far to come to the outside of this head.

Still, he goes out among you.
>Fear onions too far-a-field to come to.
>Along highway so wide
>Beneath highway untied.
>Lurks the digger of a man you were.
>In some soil, captured...*stolen*, truth tell...

What can be said in good truth anyway?

Yeah! I heard the strolling disapproval.
>You were only passing here to get to upper deck,
When in truth it were here the while.
Say I mis-trialed.

A MONSTER TOO

Oh! It's a nice bandwagon to be on,
Grant you that!
But where angel, scripture, awful and roost.
Where, "No, I will not submit all to you,
In this money sought-found foresooth."

Let me back-up a bit rightly.
have no color in mind at large.
Conceptualizing the draw you pull,
The pill, you still.

So, Ok! Most of us can only picture life as it comes,
And will admit to that!
But there are perhaps more still, who do rue, rope and rake,
You under a stroke that caught it all up that time.

This be warned of:
They who care nothing for your values depraved, or raved
about...
Voice over loudspeaker, not thine!
Walk through mire-creep, you'll find...
Wasted time granted, to these totaled, menless men mined.
Mined by those who have money to be made.
Mined by they who shall not be saved.
Will you use it, not abuse it?

EVERYWHERE POINTED

A sound-barrier break here, overhead yesterday!
A sonic boom bigger than ever heard.
Something new in the works,
Or another stealth bomber flyby.
…Worth recording here, hethinks, herewith<

Under good inspiration one can sail the moon.
Talked to Sig today, good brother what!

Let only love carry your bags over the pass.
Let only love wrinkle old tired ass.
Let only birds sing,
Trample all the lyre strings.
Make each voice one and safe.
Save this precious *global* race.

Save it from, for and to you.
Save it thumb, flap and flipper.
Forgive every sting in winter.
Stay jibe on ship of that good vigor.

Want us all to look at one another always as we see
ourselves.
Always same view in mirror more of me, more of you.
More of the blessed particular view.
Even as…a not too few, dip and dab a little
In wind of an indifference.
An indifference and removal of ourselves from Earth's
affairs,
Which leaves us howling and scratching at the door.

Let out of huge secrets, that are not.
Left out of how the precious rock…flows and allows.
Of how seas give-up and receive.
How mountains sit there and perceive.

How valleys plant well in their eves.
How desert speaks hell of reprieve.

All, tell of their master Chaos.
Cousin, good rival, Random close aside.
And sister Mistake in the parlor too.
…View good from here.
We're squinting through the delivery.
Here, we've welcomed two, no more than four good friends
home.

IN A GENERATIONAL MOOD

We know the part played by the liar.
The 'gifted' youth did not escape.
Sought prizes and accolades, like the rest.
Parents had to bail us out more than once.

Knew great minds.
Saw great deeds done daily.
Read from the most powerful books.
And your presidents and leaders were revered.

Authority got acceptance early and late, it seems.
We became fathers, while still children.
Mothers with learning plates.

Our tongues knew every new word.
Our lungs were betrayed by our vehicles,
kept meat and tree-cutting convenience turds.
We knew right from wrong once,
but those lines now blur.

Not given-up!
Saw drink spoil cup.
Saw oil-soaked sea kill fauna and we.
Saw goddesses in dreams and presents
Over and under ever tree.

Once killing was discovered, knew we wanted no more of
it.
Didn't continue praying to faces looking not like me.
Knew that The Big Guy lives in everything simultaneously.
Asked for help, drew-back veil of deceit.
Welcomed this short life and eternity both, tout a fait.

But no anger will follow there.
No regrets to tangle hair.

No causes kept covered in silent guilt-colored stares
No crying for a life lived sequestered and bare.

SAD

In the north of Cali, in a room.
Same as in any a home-town zoom.
  Would write of you if your existence were new,
  but, get too little and many too few
  instances of an adventurous social streak,
  which leads to a newness and a blues-ness.
  Nothing of interest there!

Here, can't see how it matters,
Under this arts-full Sunday of relaxation and chosen work,
This day 'of time that can let stray, be a jerk.
…Stay in doors, don't know anyone out there anyway!

Surrounded by all of civilizations advances,
Find self near-more alone now than ever.

Clubs no longer belong, so won't go there.
Dances leave a man wanting one or few good women
And a wide outdoors.

  Family all have theirs.
  And in the fate-full market, seen as a threat
  (because of a passage rite) and mostly chore.

  So what else, to do?
  Glad writing was found, this solace is mostly cure.
  Like to be a big man on campus,
  But, right at thirty on this job-market floor.

And now comes the acceptance that lords it over.
Now comes the advancement of age, of lost taste.
Taste for society is spare.
Taste for propriety is there,
But a foreign land could bring you out again.

A studio, a home, a gallery, a tome.
Walks in a forest, naps in a park.
Someone to share it with,
In full light and just dark.

LIQUID HYDROGEN

Why should we, simply being the one who takes the task…
Calling self writer, worry now, over saying so?
'Why' is question basic after 'What'.
Why is so close to survival…(here place any descriptives).
Sentence seeking and sentenced.
'Why' is akin to "What' as first thinkings,
First principles seen in that reality-place taken.

Am science fiction plundered!
…There is no arguing with something…
In some ways smarter than you, stronger than you
And coming your way.
That as you stand on the edge of a precipice, for instance.
Swoops in, attacking for the kill.

But this power does not know that *it* is food for *you* too.

The kill for you has importance's un-known by kindness.
The kill for it, instinct.

Show me your differences.
Would see them if they could be produced.
But they'll not!
For all is same, matter not the names.
…Nature's killing.

He says that the by far more complicated concepts
And answers to them,
Come from days on the plain, fording rivers,
Living till sunset, hiding in caves, escaping to mountains,
Rising of a morning, hunting, foraging, survival, belabour!

For these, the basics are never enough, never hard.
…Got at through its open port!
Taken, from cover of an underbrush.

Slipping down lee-side of its chalice cup.
Moving slowly.
Angling toward a viscous flowing up.

WHAT IT TAKES

Message light blinking on a phone in a room.
No one knows we're here, shall we bust you a tune?

Odd-man out describes it quite nicely.
Thinker weighted down by truck-load of feeling.
Introvert happy to go home of an evening.
Some cave-man resorting to hibernation as healing.

Your happy in crowds whose numbers are really
Extravagant and revealing.
Not a mobster, 'cause mobs are titanic non-feeling.

In retreat with a beer.
Glass of vodka, no tears.
Wine for your living,
Tequila! Come here!

Smoke soap in the morning.
Cook roast on the roof.
Up-standing sly weasel,
Its two tons of umf,
That will get you by,
That will successfully complete your try.

Not drink in a glass.
Not another 'great class!'
Only umf and more effort,
Only this consign thy.

CHANGING NATURE

The importance of answering the question
To your boss' satisfaction cannot be overplayed.
The absolute distinction of yourself
From those worthless dads,
Betrayed by their camaraderie, is to die for.

As a man, be a man!
As a woman, woman!
When a child at times throughout life,
Let that be!
Nature, your nature, this nature is keg!
Keg of the most powerful explosive.
Unstable, not easily handled
And supremely unpredictable.

Teach me doubtless truths that will...
Make me wake on time for work in the morning,
Make me hold family truly dear.
Help me remember choices at every tick of clock.

Train me in some mystical way.
Match my endeavors to a home-run-triple play.
Allow me to seek rightness in every conceivable fray.
Cooked my potato on the steak-skillet today!

EX-SCAPIST

Tip-toe across devils spare span of spam.
Tangle twine in hair for four, maybe five.
Memory angling for a fix.
Third night drunk into this or a similar twist.
Morphine rocket up for a mind-mist.

…Morphine rocket up for a mind-mist.
Scalawag front and bullie-bubb back.
Train bearing down this cliff-face surround.
Baby collar the dark one and make him your fist
Of vengeance and mirrored-hate specified.

Join the exciters and drunken separatists.
Clown with the part that asks why of the sky.
Say 'What' when its never, ever real dry
Outside your family fun home.
When the weather dictates the day and its gone.
When at last the art of mingling is turned to stone.

…When at last the art of mingling is turned to stone,
Lives can live in a world of mercy again.
There, welcome all the uncomfortable.
Ease minds of each frightened case.
There, write of the catch and never the chase.

Blanket-babe trapped in its helplessness sound.
Rackish blown wish bangs the castle keep down.
Official custom broken in escape from this place.
Oh Lord we've spoken!
Saint Andrew's cross, marked an 'X' on this face.

ME AND YOU

When a melancholy that entraps is discovered,
Might need to pray it away.
But watch those prayers closely,
For they may get answered.
Answered to your satisfied dis-satisfaction.

The moody specialists within will have what they will.
The arts-bound escape route is thoroughly un-bound.
The science of acceptance will be widespread
Through town and all village keeps.

Paper-chase humbug that slips nimbly on the page.
Maybe an insight's caught fast on their crooked-straight
stage.
Set with diadems and dithyrambic display.
Arms overhead, as wild cheering beckons you stay.

As on another day a swept-back wind contuses ryely.
A smile's all it takes, your consistent, timely.
Your boosted acumen for discarding distrust,
A loosened weapons list, a handhold, a thrust.

A loner sought, welcomed.
A sorry lad fuss.
Brain-dead from dissembling.
The Locusts?
A must.

SUNDAY HEREDITY

George Sand and Charles Duvernet.
Tail caught-up in his hollow, white way.
Blow a wind that crunches too…
Altruistic smashing volume.

A blue back to a white sky
These themes also wonder why.
Le' saxophone musing
The great central park.
Sylvester is losing.
We're twice light for dark.

Accepting all the chosen-fallen.
Etude relaxing in fall clothes bought taxing.
A moment remembered, a shot in the dark.

Opposites do more than attract!
They see you hung in the morning
All loose clothing tucked forever in.

As an aside…As thin as you please and a rail.
Darling you're my kind, I'm found on this trail.
May I wash you and watch you and keep you?
Will my parade pass your way?

As silence escapes round roughly,
As wakened from sleep ancient in character,
As wizened in life's fire said yes to,
Come up to your life lived in concordance with mine.
Where Countess described you as melancholic and
serious…
There I!

On wings of all birds land dreams of all herds.
On backs of writers lands scat of this earth.

A friend to live with,
A patron aboard.
And this.

OF CLEAR SILENCE

A person of silence is to be cherished!
Not spoken to quickly.
Not ignored, certainly.

All questions answered.
Pride and guilt walk nearby.
Pride of patience, guilt of omissions.
Silence unhurried is key.

Act life out! But, a carefully selected silence alone
Is revered, is verified in time…
By those who know.
By they that strive.
By a silenced questioning,
balanced waiting.

An honored silence is known;
          In the spoken word.
          dish clang.
          horrible highway.
          and mated bed.
In dreams seen leveling around a wanting head.
Not least in the confusion and ego tread.

Through casement leaped the searching soul.
Out of house finally, breaking current mold.
Studying, for instance, "Soft Internal Style of Strength".
Pushing hands mightily, altered Kung Fu clarity!

Want clarity achieved through knowing stare or smile!
Not billboards. Not lights that attract and diffuse.

I'd have the heart so true,
That if a cry escapes at lunch, at three in the morning,
Mores the better.

Oh God! For silence, for clarity!
There's the prayer.

SOME OF SEX

His door? Open to you and yours.
His moon, crusted with the pie of and estate.

>Logger-heads landed, full-bright taken to chore.
>Tonight Alice slips quiet, under slit in floor.

Movie magic noticed, trap set on the gore.
Web page encampment, bugle-busted, a more.

Long tended, to resign to the back of the room!
The rushing forward, for answers that zoom in
On the intended design...
>Running over it, in search for same.
>Cementing over, its oldest name,
>Was not for him.

He says, "Lady come here, this lap for your chair!
Fair way obtrusive, listen to your body's fine flair.
For a hand whipping across your expensive, fine dress.
For that swath in your face, with this handsome white mist.
For my taking your splendid squirt test."

Ah! Sex again!
...Yeah! And what day was that, when there was no
thought of sex?
What bay was that, where we set our caps and caught some
naps?

He's waited in this line for near thrice twelve and fourteen.
Hope we make ninety, you'all come back now, ya' hear!

A HATRED PROFOUND
(To know loss, is to know restitution, gain
and ugly compainion revenge, but this cannot make it right!)

After many beatings for a head not bowed.
In remembrance of a thousand hangings.
When mothers, daughters and the like have been ravaged.
During the time when all my manhood was told to bend,
Ask not for peace and kindness now.

After your retention of deception.
During this century of dissension,
Throw not up the bible to me.
No escape for you in this forgiveness dream.
Ask not for peace and kindness now.

When your gatherings were separated.
When you laughed in a crowd.
When the bad ones got mitigated.
When it was too late to ask how.

Look not to me for a Martinesque assurance.
Blood boils in cauldron of all these injustice turrets.
I'll kill you slowly, one by one,
Is the thought that comes.
I'll explode you slowly to kingdom's done.

Slowly, 'cause then my enjoyment and vengeance is won.
There, I follow cuttings with shots from this gun.
Where a torture is racked.
Where a hatred is backed, by a rightness that waits no
more.
By no more sermons from a supreme court floor,
By watching your face, as death knocks loudly at your
door.
Me? I'm not the nice one!
Me? I don't seek excuse!

127

There's no more understanding,
Only this eye to you.
Only teeth gnash and rye look.
Only watching to see,
…Your lie and a mob, took this life *hard* from me.
Close your eyes as I shoot first then stop.
Your sentenced in my court,
I saw your last drop and wave of a hand,
That let loose the mad ones, that jack-booted Dan.

BACK SO SOON

"William's cutting off his fingers, so they'll fit into the glove."*
Matthew's jumping from the train, to be on time for the bus.
Cindy drank tea to get drunk and John's smoked all the stuff.
20 lines or less and it's, "Hi there, I'm touched!"

A triumphant new air.
High turbulence sought there.
Malpracticed my Karate and this depth-debonair.

Local weed killing, the varmints don't care.
This bit of earth's willing to gather the fare.

It's over so soon, I missed out on so much.
The promise was kept though, I'm back in a flush.
The vortex took minutes, the float was a must.
Target?
A next life, some karma, a trust.

Line one, a quote from Tom Waits.

IN IT FIND LEAVES LILTING

This pacific harboring of Columbus' actions as commendable,
Itches all over and is not welcome.
But before loading-off in that direction...
What is dead yet not fallen?
What is native to a soil?
Only death and more death.
Only some kind of complete instant.
Only some brush with eternity outside a door.

As I conquer a land new to me, you stand by your
Well worn entrance and wonder at 'my' misery.
This traveler, this drifter, can he know a settling harmony?
Can he know the rush of joy that comes
With wife calling my name?
Is it possible to convey to him the resigned emptiness
That joins my leaving for work in the morning,
Evenings and nights?
Want only to be with family.
A simpler man is not made.
A vast gate swings wide revealing a glimpse of my heart.
In it find;
> Kindness unparalleled.
> A taste for battle, much as yours.
> A desire to live an endless young and learning life.
> The rushing forward of my loins, as I see her.
> The distance a man keeps.

It's the forcing of the issues that lose their winning!
It's the slowness of the charge that guarantees its losing!

Seeing both and all vectors as he does, leaves one looking
Long and hard and scattering.

The guy wants to write of awesome, beautifully wondrous
scenes.

DRAGONCONVERSATION
(A CONVERSATION THAT WAS NOT!)

There, with crooked designs again!
Centrist tendered mercy.
Merciful jury. What injury? What story?
What told, what found?
There! Said and welcomed.
Tread and vacuumed, caught-up in a trough, a more.
Some strokes are harsh and brad pitted.
Bi-cameral intrusion.

Oh master may we?
this house to mind comes.
Prancing over a strewn tendency
To in hollow wallow.
Where swallowing gulps of fair air,
Our hero stays stumbling, bumble-butt like mumbling
a matter thought to be sung.

So, shall I say that I am little convinced.
Or can you tell from my tone.
Are apples oranges?
Or are oranges not?

HOUSE

Weathered through decades-full discovery.
Foot falls.
Sound lifted from garden, stroke one.
Fall clothes of an evening.
Mornings? Sun broke.

POETRY

Speaking in a breathless tone.

A WORD ABOUT SENIORITY

There are memories stuck everywhere.
Here! On this shade!
Stuck to that pole.
See you in signed picture album at two?
In cracks of your sofa,
Under a chair.
Sunk deep within this carpet.
In the walls of this place.
Layer twenty-four in that road.

An earth-planted, coffin-like embrace.
A swirled miracle state.
Nine faces staring through the glass.
A non-proliferated weapons list,
A high-noon Mass.

Trashed melatonin, slashed.
A cut from the team.
Really shunt means in between so shallow
Some teens as to think they have warrant
To decide for themselves
Among the tryers supreme,
Being older than you are.

KILLING ALONENESS

Is home a home when no one marks your coming and going?
When there's no hand on the knob from the inside,
As you reach for it from the outside, once in a while?
Is a bed when only one presence is aboard?
> Well sure it is.
> But, is it a winning hand?
> Is it some well done Gantt chart
> That lays the prepared schedule out before you,
> So that now with some ease other work may begin?
Where in an aloneness the sharing and caring for another?
Where arguments that you both won't let stand.
That you crunch under foot as evening falls?

It would be a humorous beast to behold.
A numerous feast to unfold,
As wanton woman comes his way.

He, off-moment caught.
A time of proximity taught.
In which now his secrets are bought.
For full viewing sought.

We, a now broken plea.
See, our rank token sea, that flows through its ebb and tide.
That won't let our wasted hide, be that, some more.

So, shall he scrape nuts on the floor.
Perhaps a finger nail scratching a board to abhor.

I think, some poetry, to soften the randy chore.
Or, an acceptance of humanity,
Caught fast, on this off-kiltered killing floor.

ON METAL

Convinced those serving up
Strong, hard/soft, cold, brutal-based man music metal,
(Oh! Add dark and speed as inroads gained here)
are seers achieved and speaking.

They off-beat.
Top feat.

Microsoft cheat!
Is claim made by they who want surely to;
       Acquire your honed nature,
       Mis-speak its tone tonality,
       In lions-prancing mood sparingly.

As for me, still there with underdog and God as before.
Though worn, attitude walks beside
And I along side it!

Morbid nature watched and practiced
As men do all over earth.
Along-side some warrior turf,
Worth is displaced with a spry mirth.

It must bend to my calling,
Upon it and crawling, this vocabulary so (--,--_ wide.
My metal banded hide.

Encapsulated and entombed, upon a wastrel moon,
In a land once known.
As to home we traveled, bloomed, now.

WIND HE

Can now say, "seen what turns a Raven back."
Even he, the wind!
Whether female or male attributes are given
To a thing, a phenomenon, an entity like wind,
It cannot be sung enough.

It cannot be turned away, by a rotten breakfast
With a rotting kin.
Nor by toddling adventure with gin-toddy gin.
Nor can wind...be stopped successfully from
Coming out of your little tiny ass
A tiskit, a taskit!
Go on and try it!
Your Carlucci diet!
Um! Never kept quiet!

ENIGMA

We spoke of a Martinesque assurance as applied to its
opposite.
Now we do same of an Eastwood-like banking many
women,
Untamed, untied!
Many children besides.
In this you have access to your multiple self.
Tagging alongside a prosperity in this access and
proximity,
Which is combination to the safe
Which is mans only chase
Have money, have fame, have woman.

Now we have, "Thank you very, very much!"
Let tons approach wicked/straight thought houndings,
Taken too far afield to be of use to us in these foundings.

A *breathing* heads-up display.
Tibetan monks screened.
There books careened, by some Chinese screams.
In it find - made up, out of a TLC weekend.
A TLC learning weekend?

And you are disagreed with, in this going to other lands
And there, taking out of their bit of earth,
Your backyard stolen worth.
Leaving death in your throws
Looking back only to prepare your stuff for shipment.
For my clipment, when accounts are stricken and taken to
ease.
For your coming stand of tethered earth.

A sprout of information grown.
A tangent quotient, a locked-back knife edge.
A bolts of lightening pledge, potions swallowed, fed.

139

COUNTING SHARES

Happy writing now.
Writing happy, how?
Rampant classic sows, being a
breed of crazy cows.
Maple street the case, South
Central bleed the face.
You've exported your brand of
gangsta' hip,
a gangster flip-chart enclosed, so
they could…pick
red or blue.
So that two, count them two,
anyones slip on peel
left out to steal a soul and body.
Maybe Windsor castle will give back what was
stolen, but not
Burned.
Le' Hermitage or the Louvre will give back,
what was alternately stole and earned.
Perhaps Cairo can have a few mummies
back.
Oh! Mommies back Alfred! Now you'll fry
like a loon!
Separate tabs from expectant warm soothe!
Fire-up rab on protected hot oooze…
An oooze like nationality
or wicked country this way comes!
A loose-tooth gathering,
smiles wretched, welcome cuz!

If you tell me you like no one very much, that does
not look like you,
I'd welcome said conversation, I'd make picture of
the view.
If you tell me you like me as much as I like you,

140

may leave at sunset, nothing left to que
another land needs me now. Angels yet wonder how
we came and went under such a shunned-out view of our
worth.
Wonder why we hung in, why not tare-up the earth?
As retribute we packed down that turf and covered over (as
much as we could)
a soil that wants exclusion, seeing in that illusion and in
that no mere fusion
of self to self, but a series of well-hung shelves,
where we could collect and redirect the missing feelings.
Feelings still bare in a have and keep it all street-fare,
a free-wheeling corporate think-chair,
a vastly empty then, human share.

WHAT FLOWS

A fluidity seems to be at work in our world, that girders all.
A selectively timed viscous array.
Smoke-stack lifting, 'Earthen floor' sifting.
There are buttes that move, plates and continents that slide
And sand and waterway that know not what else to do.
You find spar-ed rock flows, tree wind blows,
Blood and chlorophyll (one molecule off) veins racing.
Clouds that pass on their way to a heavenly dripping.

Religions that talk of life-force whipping about.
Can you see it?
Can you feel it, taste it in your mind?
Can it be all good or is it most unkind to our human sleep?
Find and taste it in your being!
Being the being that you are.

Time flows and is sharp.
Cuts a mighty figure, stops and starts.
Air is quite viscous, makes art and sport of us.
Science and philosophy are controlled by speed…
Speed of understanding and waiting to see.
Speed of new insights and much hang-man controversy.

Light and dark know only each other!
Light travels at a defined rate!
Sound and vibration seek constant escape.

The tears that wash the orb.
Snot that hits the floor.
Clothes that pass their way.
Food down throat and beyond.
Gravity tugging at this arm.
A flowing vault of 'I".
Only His reasons why, yet the simplest is the hardest.
Yep! This 'god' is the artist!

STOPPED DOWN

I can help you little, in your quest to be more, see?

From forest deep like thee.
And to be from there is to shout it out, nearly everywhere.
As others do!
Forest is desert, rock, farm, soil…
Any and all these, more!
My staccato Monk move.
Soothing beast tendered belly parts.

And the trajectory twixt the straight
And the Coltrane line is straight!
Ya gotcha 'Big Nick' floatin' around up there somewhere!
These men, like non-white baseball teams,
Men of strong construction too
Like men-folk in my family, were living,
On extreme end of hero

Sandy-shore leave never given,
Only taken like the white do,
Like the kite do, when relieved of its tether.

GETTING CLEARER

This is how the conversation started,
"Dad, Do you buy stocks, I mean corporate notes?"
Why, yes son, I do!
Dad, do you cause Old-growth forests to be taken down
Burned for coal, drilled for oil in?
Do you Dad, allow native peoples, people with
A land of their own, to be displaced, run-off,
resettled.
And Dad, have you allowed this to go on for how long
now?"

Give me a chance son!
If your asking, whether or not I 'OK' every move
A company I have bought into makes, then no,
I do none of those things.

"Dad, by posing that question as a kind of defense,
You've marked yourself a guilty shareowner."

Son, don't be so serious!

A PROPER DIMINISHMENT

Its what he knows about himself,
that estranged him from others.
It's about those stupid little lies
that got trapped in tellings from time to time.

That he knew diminished him mightily,
that now hunt and haunt him occasionally.
Sit in classrooms, strewn to the walls.
Learn a lot!
But do never forget, that all untruth
As simple as it is, gets stuck in craw
And easily drawn out.
For…air 'neath a mountain so wide!
"Entombed!", says the watcher nearby.
"A line at, a thought at, a time to you."

To you too, nice empty quarters of the house,
to set up studio (for a bout of sculpting, painting, the like).
To catch some nearby's moving by!

Moving toward mostly *quiet* room,
that extended moving garden,
from one house to another.
Some awful charter, quiet murmur.
Some 'telling frost' and 'tepid noose'?
Only a living, foresooth!
Fore and aft,
a lively craft he has, to carry his load of
disgust, misuse, hard rebuttals,
harsh recommendations, mangled *me* too.

He does it because he must…continue to move
toward this screaming, hand-waving warning at self.
To never again in years and lives ahead…
Never again take and make so much of self.

M I B

Having gotten off to a tremendous start,
Shall we now remove to another galaxy?
One in a tube. in a globe. Hung on a chain.
Around a neck. Of a being. In a world, that is not?

Fodder main is video and film noir!
Found 'de Bergerac, Sand, and more!
Drowned in a senior luck pool.
Following freshmen on toilet-seat-stool.

Doctor sculpture, written chore.
Assault scripture never more.
Flounder might and main, 'gainst baton-door.
Hatches are uncovered, sweating whore.

'Tying self to ship; headed beyond these shores',
May cause mis-functia altruistica.
Which thing, wouldn't want pinned to my chest!
Which zing got your best?
Made you stop, stand up in mid-track and sweat?

MISSION STATEMENT

To persuade and dissuade.
To open so many possibilities
That near non-movement prevails.
…As crippling effect curtailed.

WHAT LIKED, WHAT SEEN

Not yes people.
Not consistently no.
Only those open to the people show,
shown on the screen many times are.
Seen on the street a short story below.
Watched while your cubicle walk was displayed.
Flown with through the air.
A sentenced stayed. Where?
Not simple wanting.

Seen in your 'blue steel and thunder'.
Ideas integral to your design.
Slanted eyes.
Rounded hollow ones.
Ones that have wonder written over them.
And those that seem narrowed by a coming, on-rushing
event.
In the kitchen seeing the making of the feast.
With a sister at a grave with its sweep.
A wide swath with dread hand.
Tallied bliss with loves like this.

Beings stratified.
Opened wide.
In their wake a flipping cape-a-pie.
A sweeping dry dust flying.
Mission about.
A plying.

Praises sung whilst trying.
Buying none of your third act,
in here with me now, what is this?
Fish sprang from polluted pools,
into those with light and dark hiding places
and some food when needed.

For a living!
For a swimming!
And all this happened in the blinking of an eye.
And wonder why, I tell it!

WHAT HE DID AND DID NOT WEAR

The narrowing was expected, but not this harrowing
amazement.
Not, read another great artist or scientist and know abilities
abandoned.
Again, it's the turn of a phrase, the saying of the thing your,
his, her way.
That variety that just keeps on coming.
Untested depths and reserves.
Un-chested knocks of a turn..
A barrel of mischief, this mystery earned.
Staring back across your queer abyss
Your young French twist, a Rimbaudian dismiss.

If a writer keeps you there for hours, what words can be
said,
To describe for he who knows not, the joy of a book.
Not a tortured following of books in a book
His words mis-took, no!
The writings of those who are they excised.
Self blown to bits, by a rightful ritualized...
Cabin in the hills where lac and stream meander
through a dream.

Then, that 'Rune of irrestibility' that followed you
everywhere.
That was ever barely there.
Tucked close to your vest, in a nook in a chest,
What a sanded desktop rest.
Yeah! Sit your sweet female ass, next this breast of mail
Armour lain past the entry to bedroom blest, full!

Let a book be hailed as history's lesson.
Let words spoken be left on the dais as they entered.
Not now, have need of a morbid lecture!
Not then did hide from the sister rector.

Nor the father praying and bottles draining
As *that* wine flowed.

Saw pores feed as a nose was squeezed.
Saw Mom's feet same as these.
Dad's hair, seeming white birth seized.
Animal earth inside a pair of jeans.

ODYSSEY

Came through it, only halved.
Could have been worse, was fortunate!
Other travelers did not fair as well!
Crows might have gathered and sat above door.
Dogs and cats could easily have trained.
Might have lain in the low grass and completely
disappeared.
Ennui could have made them hers, that day in May, when
distracted.
If ears were tuned to your discourse, could be a wastrel
now.
In those grosser days, could easily have killed.
What was watching over?
Why only trip, not fall?

When night first showed herself, could have been brave,
But in retrospect, 'twere best, was scared.
As mothers and fathers fell to their knees, I screamed
profanities too!
I blocked out the sun on those first days,
Then thinking better of it, moved aside.
Flowers always bloomed in my indoors.
Outside, mirrors were shades of a following.
Bought tickets to all dark concerts,
Bashed my head-bangs against any standing wall.
Stood just right of stage left.
Moods? In the billions.
Nothing I said in houses rang true in forests.
Never once sang with the choir. Oh, was there,
But mouth did not move.
Lost to agony built on ruins of some religion cared for
at the time,
simply sat down and waited.
As time passed on edge of these tracks, derailment was evident.
Every wasted hour danced and laughed before as sank.

153

Took head-patting advice you gave and eyes teared.
When last left to teach, was pedantic, sorry!
Motorcycle rides? Heavy, strenuous and tardy.
Laughed in places specified for cries.
Put tongue in there too.
Every word ever uttered was too loud and hurt ears.
Could have been a comic, but past got in the way.
On those varied occurrences when books acted like movies...
stretched imagination 'til, rubber-band-like, slapped
awake.
By forgetting to, 'protect my appetite and my loves',
damned self to this rising consciousness.
As my scientific method broke through doors and windows
And would not behave, as it came in with the dust that
landed
Everywhere...muse, it seems decided I was not in love and
strayed.
Never admitted this before but, can hear angels and devils
whisper.
Mounting and riding a captured beast, became annoyed
and dare I say
bored.
Tooled up, suited up, rushed forward, slept in dank
basements,
Contracted malaria, caused islands to blow.
No one ever got close enough to see these eyes glow.
Studies in anthropology lost importance as the ships
landed.
Tapped into a perilous precipice twice.
Lingered behind every arched entry, whether coming or
going.
No mysteries were quite as mysterious as one part of this.
I buttoned buttons, zipped a zipper or two
And almost always cried in the soup.
Blasting caps and marinade made equal impression.
Toyed with disaster and clamped-down the matter.
If you saw me as impatient then, it was mirage.

In middle passage, took heads, shrank them to manageable size
and the game of marbles was born.
When rope was offered, cleaned fish and hid.
Louis, Charles, Ludger and Joseph are names that seek.
This hat has wide brim and catches mist.
Learned from every lyric.
Just upon sitting at table, cornucopia walked away.
Largess cannot be ascribed.
Fumbling, I stand firm.
Humbling this mind turns…into a triangular marsupial course,
Where jumping is forbidden and leaping is de 'rigor
And 'll not argue the differences with ya here.
Lately, printers have given-up their art.
Part of tangle is new Dre(a)d-Scott angle,
Offered up as subliminal.

Still, through it all, manage the courage to sit as pee (at home).
I have to clean it!
Ask God to hear a tattered, constant plea.
And speaking of love as principle in nature; bend bar,
Stroke tee, answer no one, welcome thee.

AN ANGRY RELINQUISHMENT

When last I looked, was angry enough deep inside,
about perceived reception,
to cause all your damns to bust, spill blood, guts
and sinew all over you.
Was so full of those head-shaking glances,
saw miles of heads skewered to poles along highways.

Need a severe stepping back here!
Need to lose this nine to five hurried decay.
need to let you have your day, month and year without me.
See what that does for your superior method of display,
For your tilted eyes and blanko way.

When I calm down, I'll still be endlessly concerned about
my attitude.
I'll still want to hold hands and walk you through my
perceptions.
Want to cal it all right and okay and put what good
construction
I can on the thing.
Want to avoid the rot, impatience, anger.

But time narrows for a peace council!
War cry stuck in roof of mouth!
And unless I shout it out, I'll be unable to swallow next
meal,
Thus sustain my existence, which is key to me,
Which is hell to you.

Not careful now about what said!
If I come through this, I'll be glad you hate me.
Monotone calm is thoughtless amazement and blessed spot!

When last I breathed an easy breath, think I was nine!
Maybe seventeen was a really good year.

Perhaps where I am now; disgusted, wired, worried, feeling captured,
is your idea of heaven, but not mine.
Perhaps retirement is another kind of hell.

Having seen other hells and heavens, good and bad days,
almost don't want to play anymore.
You win!

LITTLE CHAOS

Ageless disparity.
Insouced anachronym.
John Leonard would not have it,
but…thou too, art like some god of a Sunday Morning.
With what language a tale is told.
What studied assurance,
what ease of difficult not, delivered.

While looking in other direction…
That one stranded day, you remember it!
One in which you gleaned,
maybe you *are* consigned to this
Auger Enforcement.
This twisting while turned.
This that is done.
This being held from above.
A clue to nothing Despite your trying,
this formula too will go the way of Occam's Razor,
Liking 'better' improvisation with its structure, simple!
A little chaos going a long way

Too, on some weekend day quite some time ago…
sorted out whole slew of 'guarded gates'.
Loitered about an empty chasm,
and saw clouds do things, clouds ought not.
Two of my pocket watches joined the leaving ships crew.
I ran, half awake, through five or so wasted evenings in a
few fogs.
Algorithms by the threes, came to the dance, dancing
across the lawns,
stamping-down the new-grown heather,
that laid lounge-act satisfied moments before.
Pity!
Then, danced along a filtered pianos nuance and break.
Wondered out loud about Sir Francis 'California' Drake.

Never would bow down, except that now, it is a must.
And so, as he apologizes to his tormentors for being victim,
releases into this already mixing soup a new nullification,
one that accepts what it does not.
and wrangles with the rest.

NoT tO nAmE

A bond of physics entered handbook.
Block of marble, maple syrup.
Took a chew on me hat yesternoon.
Killings of a plan crash, rice worn.

Few hours loose, as we wait for the train.
(got too much clothes on from night before).
What is a mans relation to his shadow?
Is it only the throw of light?
Or is it more?
Maybe (he says again), it is too, like the splitting of white light.
Perhaps it is a side-of-beef, of you.
A slice cut, another angle found,
that reveals innumerable more ideas to test,
inroads that best describe our desired keen attempts at
discovery.

Then, in timely fashion let us see the new merchandise.
Spy through those trees for first light.
stay in the valley till a half past three
There! That tree should line-up with yon ridge from where you
now stand.
See it?
Move not! Till you see the signs!

And you took it on faith.
Waited successfully for the gate to open,
and it did. And there was awe and conscription and being
used,
fairly tooled for sets of chores, all accomplished.
You satisfied, other satisfied.
Now only a parting.
Teacher and student taken up in said process.
Hands across chest, hands not akimbo.
Perhaps goodby!

TILTED #2

He tells them,
"Don't tell anyone else I might be coming,
don't look for me
and don't worry if I don't call."
He says this as if it mattered
yae! matters.

It does and doesn't!
(Not simply caught posing opposites!)

If you make bold enough in your analysis
to think you have broken on the promise
answered the question you were paid to answer,
then maybe you have.
But forget not the others part and play.
He that would climb, must be prepared to fall.
It is no secret minor part, an a-taxment!
It is voice over radio that shins,
as though it had just arrived from some nineteen-forties.

A connection to times past is so close to us all, each!
Memories launched after query.
A bringing-up.
There, on the screen!
Ah, now! Divide three and four to their saved quadrants!
yes! Leave one and two where they lie.
Lime is not necessary say some to concrete.
But try it without and the Roman & Greek will willow and weep.
Set stone and stone in possible spaces.
yet moan and moan for empty faces.
Blank stares withstanding,
this yank bears some watching.

Spanked his baby, 'cause she asked for it!"
Yanked his bone, to the regulated.

One such as he, would need women that were used to men.
Not these American novices.
Not easily these totalitarian princesses, wrapped-up in their idea
shoelaces, tangling with a moried, standing beast.

DARE YOU FEEL INVITED?

Sat in sun for a few days straight now.
Learned this…extent of effort, dictate extent of rest,
when no external force is preventing same,
looked yearningly for bushels of flowers, herbs, leaves,
pine cones, stalks, twigs, the like.
After which, swept-up ashes, laid new fodder,
made fires' place secure.
Fooled no one.
When sun feels as if its stinging-burning, it is!

What did you learn down there?

Learned no one cares very much for truth!
They'll not back your warrant!
There'll be no affirmed actions there!
No shackling, but no entry either.
And why do you think that is?
Because you've brought nothing to the game,
to table…you created what?
man-plasted be-ravements on all sides!

Apple of eye, his eye, her eye, his.
Loaded-up with knowings and non-purple art-museums.
After Vivaldi, Michealangelo, Beethoven and Edward are
taken to task,
for interjecting their valued worth,
for mightily upsetting our 'warrior turf'…and all else,
('Twas harmless and a good time!).
We are found back on the twenty-third eastern shore with
our captured
mellow-minds. Thinking this is what it was all for, all
about.
A quick journey and these.
My comfort and ease!
A twittle-twat squeeze. Make you gush like an orbit.

Make you flow like a body. Lady forget tidy and timing.
Be 'grown out' of propriety and guard,
Let you hang out, all over my house!

This loading-up the cupboards with a family living,
is the thing to do, when it is!
This leaving any tendency toward another breath, beat,
mind or eye,
is welcoming, come try!

AS THIS AMERICAN..

Bellicose actions.
Twisted turns in the sky.
Ramble and raggle, its here and it's why.
It sought you out not!
You came for it.
Happiness does not know it exists!
It does not know its opposite does not exist.
Blind to so many superfluities, like anything carrying
dichotomy,
many of the things that do not matter are not known to it.
Wisdom is this way too.
It gives not any kind of a crap,
for this or that or for wrong or right,
nor really for any jilted, stopped and sullen song.
Subtract not smiling, warned and savvy czar-ian.

Wanda's worryin'.
Adele may be sorry, orientating the last few contacts.
I'm guessing, 'cause I don't know!
I'm testing all the latest from the electronics supershow!
Beamed up hastily, gazing on outward blow.
Lined-up *applied* not quality concerned.
A fix needed then not now. Affixed. Affirmed.

A man leans in with heart and chin.
And it is right!
European front,
to African back.
I tell this!
With the way in which these peoples (in large) have
suffered
through all the crazy hatches, lifting out onto rotten waking
worlds,
(had enough of those)…with the way this has gone on…

One wonders at how the sun leans in the evenings.
Shudder only, thinking of going on like this.
We grab a couple more hand-fulls and sack-down for the
night.
When waked, it is to a transmissioned amazement,
lain low in annals of our wireless gazement.
The channels were hundreds like promised.
We took charge of ourselves and sifted through those filed,
retrieved, then filed again Swahili-French-Russian-Chinese
conventions.

A WRITERS QUARTERS

Said you wouldn't do this again,
'til greatly inspired.
But no! Think you want to see what will come otherwise.
Over shoulder, gliding over roof.
Coming in through walls, angling just past ear.
There, through finger and key to paper, page.
Over Zeus' head.
There! Nothing but you?

Yes I see it! But am I to be elated?
And is it only you?
Shall I be happy for you, who have no ear to bend?
What shall they make of this honored stone you carry,
this dreamy stand?
…Seen by some as burden, by others…blessing.
By you…as clearly both, with their separations
most days, barely discernible.
That they wash over and interrupt each others speech is certain.
That you are careened, toppled and set on head is usual.
That dichotomous suffering beckons.
that you see not even ground for trees,
as though your walk were angelic and non-earth touching.
As your efforts make you barely a farthing.

In this mode, one banked the flow and brought down the
marshes.
Thanked Santa, sent home the cautious.
A tendency to strangle the helper and bring home the beast,
is where we are in this fondling, clutching, rapt and sliding,
quoxing him to life, writers dungeon.

Lo! Perhaps too much is made of this risen folly.
Yo! Simple touch is right match, Holly!
Take time to set down broach.
With ample office, moment approach,

167

Let wing fly and mountain stay.
Land in air…all things stage.

RELATIVITY

Quiet, most quiet!
Helped with life.
Scalped by no knife!
Accepted in pew,
Waffling in que.
Clouds cover darker parts!
Any silence suspected, hails from a cross-town park.

Mobil feasts and ratted-out peace,
alternately coming.
Lain low by crusted foresail, that could not fail.
Built to *tackle* the sea,
But, built by you and me.

Every movement under tarp is good for the gander.
If you would be sharp, gather locks, not heather.

Sharp enough by choice, to go south with the matter.
(Or north if it called for it).
Off with the head, then bleed the live body, faster, faster.

Token of what as youngster once was!
Coasted, with one foot off pedal, through all of this!
And laughed and sighed, eaten toughened hide.

Hard-tack made too close to the fire.
Apples and pears leapt last, sired others of kind
and lasted easily through worst of times.

Maintained absolute in a restrictive relative-ease.
Got 'round to a big one, in space of a flea.

FOLLOWING COURSE?

Now said, we'll move on to larger quarters.
Basements same as lofty boarders.

       Pants put on, one leg at a time.
       It's comforting to know. It's right, it's fine.

Slabs of dry verse.
Tabs made out of this mirthless wonder we've become.

       Stayed housed in the ships focsle.
       Forward with crash and mock of the sea.

In it, a touted variety.
Hailed propriety.
Stay tuned, you'll find your lost and wasted anxiety,
That comes in with the muse,
That is tattered, abused.

       Form monotone with hand not quite waving.
       Let them clap looking and shaking.

Now home to a broken, soft tendency,
To climb on roof and goof-up what pleasantry
Came by association with your name.

       Is it quite the same?
       A smothered claim, forced in these ears,
       Washed with eight tears, that hid from the refrain.

Your costs and your revenues are yours.
Goal too…speak through the voices-a-blur.

A JUMBLED MESS

You said that, "at the end of an era, fact and myth are indistinguishable!"
How does this apply?
Saved yourself from that sibling society.
Became an adult despite it all.
No moments seized, only beckoned lightly.

Satiated himself through this holiday season.
Came clear of pushed-forward excuses and empty reason.
Tried heavily to take back the mean,
Dropped coins in your pouch,
See! He's a part of the team.

Tell enough, of this didactic misery, feigned to no degree pomposity,
Rotund absentry.

So shun usury, flake your potato when its done.
Shake cake and batter, upset ovens et al.

Won prize, handed out, at back of stage.
A month ago there would have been none of this,
We were here. We held...what reins?
Our kingdom flown to bits for what, for this?

If I can't stop you from coming in,
I'll ask that you stick your head in that trough...yeah! Just there!
And with that off...off...off, or!

Perception and reality too, are indistinguishable.
When loaded-up on trivia and seek-wired give-,me-everything-ea.
Tie that in!
That bit of cloth will do fine to stop-up the metal!

How many dikes have been entered, breached sonny?
How many times did I build too close to the river!
Why-docked self and all listening.
Got up to good stuff in wishing fair, robust jubilations to
you bursting!

A page takes on it's own order.
I'm here, that's all I can say!
I'm near! I fear jeopardy!
And wounded-knee massacres

FOR GIVE ME SIR! 'RIDING FOR THE BRAND'

A tattered misery!
Take this coming conflict over a number of intolerance's,
for instance!
It may be an evolutionary necessity.
It may, in fact, be a given, conceded to by this universal
consciousness,
That wants and does not, want it!
There are times when looking in your eyes,
clear signs of hatred are perceived,
(not interested in making hay of the stuff,
The information is as tool for increasing...)
There are times when seeing you, ancient territorial
responsibilities
Are felt tugging at sleeve.

These old, reptilian feelings, show pictures of you
writhing in pain
...dying, in this cartoon, while I look on relieved.
As said, I want this and don't want it and I don't think that
you hate
Constantly either, but...
Become pessimistic about our ability to stave off this
looming disaster.

Thinking that more than anything...

It has to do with our societies desire to sustain
What cannot be sustained and harriously maintained.
And that is this over-use and waste.
We had better!
Our Louis L'Amour,
Our Jed-like Michael Latching!

STOCK

Too charred to call her now.
Knowing what will be said,
Will give no chance to be blasted away.

This predicament is not just mine!
When the world in which you live has been unjustly
assigned,
When you want else and it's so hard to find...
Stay clear on the mission.
Take stock of the stuff,
Early in the morning, stamp-out rough parts
And vie for every plus.

In a fog, a haze.
Through non-drug induced phase of altered perceptions
And meanings not yours,
Find, hold and share...this, the true helpers air...

Hell! More impossibilities!
Holding air?
What stupidity and tremulous timidity.

Yes! That's it! That's what will be performed I' the sweet
heat,
Of calling your name, the chanced sameness of the game,
That is not a game.

If you knew where you were going with this,
You would go there!
Accompanying amazement is seatingly found.
Where open ear is bent, by what might be profound.

YOU ARE

A gambler, a calculated risk taker.
A caution thrown to the wind,
A reckless abandon guy.
Malpracticed socialist.
Coffee and tea drinking stuffy.
A clock watcher.
Trouble stalker.
Field-glass spyer.
Communications buyer.
Needed brother.
Reluctant father.
An even worse grandfather.
A son with wrinkled eye.
In short a *regular* guy.

You're a type underclassed,
Some high-society trashed.
Low enough to know why,
But too satisfied to try.
Cognizant of every debate,
But it looks as though you'll only wait.
Introvert mostly, but extrovert now.
Anthology signed and wondering how.

Take supper in the evenings and sit through the mess.
Wash dishes before leaving, it's a helpmate test.
Assigned to your living like leaves on a tree,
Despite any giving, it's goodby to thee.

In last few years you've been welcomed home
About ten times.
That's ten more than usual and hundreds less than wanted.
Reversion to sadness is handed to you chief.
You clutch it to bosom as though it weren't cheap.
Making much of little and worrying to teeth,

Your sold on your living,
An archaic, progressive feat.

HOVERER (CRUSTY OLD DUDE)

A new folder.
New feat.
Some parked yardage within which to meet.
Blank stare ripped-off and put in pocket.
Defenseless, standing, awful, rocket!

Twas more reasoned, the other view!
Twas why, who, where, what and few.

You knew that was coming and either care not!
He swung 'round to meet him, the arm broke a lot!

More caution and things tried
More strength in the air
More traveling to heights, when there's no one else around,
A head and body that is unity wanting.
Where trying to summon up some distant, distinct ancestor,
That's too long hovering, we said...

Fire flows too, but only when hot enough.
Those principles again...Thermodynamics
More viscous array! No chance to stray, from nature!
More moment caught!
Strobe light bought.
"Messenger!   Side step!", "Yep!   You missed it, (--,--) just
much."

Side-stepping through what muck and oft admired mire.
Put evidence in hand, stroking back from liar!

Matter moment, matter matter, shucks!
Matter voicious, not vicious, shut-up!

Baby! Don't ask me to follow any particular view
On any particular day, or hour, or such.

PERSPECTIVE

Johnny thought aloud, "When wine has left the glass,
What will the glass do?
As a foolish hand leaves the warmth of a pocket, does
pocket
Long for its return?
When comb or brush has served well and is tossed aside,
Does it feel pain or loss?

I know the dog pines for my return.
Cat could care less!
Canary is helpless without me.
Mice? Well, their work is never done!
Spiders in rafters are quite independent.
Not one of my tools or utensils have a will of their own.
Blind bats see through hills.
Nab and bag that one Pete, there's soil to till!"

Waited endearingly to stand on line for your show.
As we passed each other unnoticed,
Moon let out a sigh and relieved now, smiled on,
(even though we could not see it).
Mounds of opinion stacked-up
Dry eyes had to be legislated against.
And mornings were not passe'.

We needed three squares like they used to care about the
environment!
Oh, for green packaging and labels and food!
I hate every last one of them! Look what they left us.
To have been so selfish, so unknowing, so uncaring.
To have been so blind, to have given us no thought!?
Wish I could bring them back from their desecrated graves,
To see this, to see what we don't have!
An article came over the ScapeNet today,
That describes how they wasted resources.

That kind of abandon has to be the greatest evil!

Well, on a more upbeat note! I'm told a new kind of fungus was
discovered at test depth and they say its quite delicious!
But the matter is not solved!

THEN AND NOW

Left boot lashed to a wall outside.
Weighed-in on all previous opinion and was tolerant.
The usual exceptions? Ruled 'still effective!'.
Many phrases thought to be clever, were revealed of their
sameness.
Altostratus decided to become altocumulus just like that!
Cloisters cloned themselves. Challenged by your meaness,
Cloudland-like, I compose my own scripture.

Told to read something new and exciting, chose a 19th
century French
Writer and have yet to look ahead!
Now charge affluence with the missing pieces, that have puzzle
In such disarray.
Belly full and mind stifled.
Telling you is a blind sightful.
Mixing pleasure with anger and pain with verse,
Enter cathedral precisely quite terse!
And lonely enough, we scrape for this feast.
Looking twice for the caterer, we're okay with these
Few pieces of pie and tostada surprise while circled by
fullness
of asking why.

Whilst in a languid safari mood,
We bank all our money and call them the fools.
They who save not, they who save at all.
The formula are random, luck the tool.

Prepare your self for the meeting, its sad.
Stay lost in own thoughts, its old, its bad!

Cid, a Queensland water dropping!
These days are frot with questions asked flopping.
Tried opting in, then out.

Sly-stoned also!
Strode sideways, as lateness wore off.
You analytical Lipper, Seed-like ripping.
Cavuto snipping.

OVER THE DIN

I know! Watched you for two days now!
You're not angry, not moved.
Don't care for chance to…get words in edgewise,
                  make feelings known,
                  bring us back from the brink,
                  rescue our process. Disgusted!

We sought not your input. Thought you were silent,
because you had
Nothing to offer.
How now, we see the error of our ways!
How cloudy was our gaze!
Could have dropped this issue too in out-basket,
Done!

But, you did not rush-in, were not loud enough,
We did not know you were there!

You were not prepared to compete for attention,
Din was culprit and effect.
We passed over you, did not hear your start.
Clearing throat, you called out speakers name,
But, the shouters, the impression makers, were all
powerful!

They clipped off your moment.
Made you think better of what input you might have lain
At foot of this altar.

I know! You say you will never compete with others,
To show intelligence.
Could never see yourself shouting over crowd.
Your ideas are better than gold,
Quietly contemplated of old

And wanted, but sold…for pittance, and a ranting, chin-climbing soul.

Never think all ranters don't care.
They simply must be shouted away.

Some souls assert only as a must!
Let not answers and decisions be taken only by those impressed
By their towering voices and soap-box prowess, used badly.
Lest right thinking and an intuitive common sense be lost.
Lest your humble input be the reason and the cost.

SHORT SHRIFT

How to rebut, "Revise, revise, revise!" as advice to poets given?
Can't!   But, do not suggest doing away with the thing that got
you there!
Twas up in front!
Face forward and tarring, but sustained of finding!
Blowing off, in this wind!
Finding, finding!

Blinding, blinding!
Write like this…First. Write!

What? You waited a moment there!
What was that? Did you think there was more?
Did you see something, feel something? Smell something?
Would ask me, who have little clue?
Save self and other. And he screeches-out he and she!
And two of these appear.
Did mean to *not* capitalize on the thing, of the proposed reason!
Shied rid, of smoking broken leaves shy-shifted,
And blasted off latest moon assigned to those challenges.
Me Sensei is ominous.
He's she, everywhere, in everyone and there!

'Doors closing, across a glen!'
Shows shorty more 'sorry!', while hand makes thee win.
And now you want, - good or bad - taken-up?
Not I!
Lost thgere before!
Would we gather up our three or four hundred differences
And after weighing them, find ourselves firmly resolved.
To take only what is given and waste not a measure?
Eat a little, like a lot.
Eat when hungry, exercise, find it! Out there!
Shi.. Twice or more a day…depending upon,
Trunk twists, punches, pulls, sit ups and downs, standings,

knee bends,

Running-in-place. I'll not ruin the page with this!

You'll not break out the sage and smoke up the room.

Follows zoom with room as a fun happening with short-shrift shallowing,

       'neath war-torn peddling. Edifying, reveling.

INTERVIEW READ!…

………………………………..

Rd-QS-in.: … "That is all!"

       They bow facing Earth and both Seti Prime and the Sentinel disappear.

ABOUT THE AUTHOR

Joe Duvernay has been "at" poetry for about 20 years now. (His first book included writings from the early 1980's.) Through this time he feels he's been able to set down to some degree his emotions, etc.

He is father to 5 adult children and two previous books of poetry: "I Begin" (Poems, Essays, Thoughts, and Observations) and "Offering."

10243090R00115

Made in the USA
Monee, IL
25 August 2019